GROWING UP ITALIAN AMERICAN

MEMORIES-CUSTOMS-HERITAGE

by

JOHN M Di BiASE

authorHOUSE™

1663 LIBERTY DRIVE, SUITE 200
BLOOMINGTON, INDIANA 47403
(800) 839-8640
WWW.AUTHORHOUSE.COM

First published by AuthorHouse 02/01/05

ISBN: 1-4184-5540-7 (e)
ISBN: 1-4184-4374-3 (sc)

Library of Congress Control Number: 2004092202

Printed in the United States of America
Bloomington, Indiana

This book is printed on acid-free paper.

Dedicated
To
My wife
Rosina Di Biase
Proud mother of six

GROWING UP ITALIAN AMERICAN
(Memories Customs Heritage)

Introduction

Immigrants from the Mezzogiorno southern part of Italy arrived in Buffalo to give economic opportunity and freedom to themselves their children and grandchildren. Nine stories from the 1930's and 1940's bring to life their labors, joys and sorrows, as well as the food they ate and wines they made. Come laugh, sing, eat, cry with us in memory of our parents, grandparents and the heritage they gave us.

Characters in stories
are from black outlined
Italian Mezzogiorno
Regions

color

Table of Contents

Introduction vi

Chapter 1 Shoemaker Peppino 1

Chapter 2 Strong Hands Mason Manoforte 11

Chapter 3 Panzanillo Polo and the Pull Chain Toilet 32

Chapter 4 Stumbluccis' Disgrazia, A Letter Regarding 48

Chapter 5 Instigatore Sarto 75

Chapter 6 Un'occhio 93

Chapter 7 Squagliacum 113

Chapter 8 Filomena Bue 141

Chapter 9 Mr. Georgio and Peppino 163

About the Author 183

Chapter 1

Shoemaker Peppino

Fuori!   *Fuori!*   *Fuori!*

Manoforte, Sarto, Un'occhio, Squagliacum, Stumblucci, Panzanillo, and Filomena Bue reacted to the definite demand of Peppino, who ordered everyone out of his shop. Gallo, being his usual feisty alcoholic self, was about to argue with Peppino. Before he opened his mouth Manoforte grabbed the upper arm of the bowlegged, lightweight, with his heavy, mason-calloused hand and walked Gallo persuasively out of the shoe shop. As the men and Filomena Bue walked out they shared no voice. Intrinsically they understood, individually separated, and went home.

Peppino had these attacks occasionally. When they occurred, he needed complete quiet. Ordinarily he enjoyed laid off workmen being in his shoe shop during winter months. Usually, he could tolerate and even enjoy the laid off laborers socializing and warming themselves in his shop. Not all, but some *Amici* (friends) worked seasonal construction jobs during warm weather as laborers. Gallo worked all year round as a street cleaner for the city of Buffalo, starting at 5:00 AM and usually finishing by noon.

Peppino reasoned that he had to pay for the heat anyway. During the depression, it didn't make sense to waste heat only on himself.

His shop was a place for sociability, conversing in Italian dialects, but no card playing or *la morra* was allowed. After a short time, all of the *Amici* understood each other's dialects.

Gallo (rooster) always favored Mussolini for invading and mustard gassing the people of Ethiopia plus he made the trains run on time. Gallo was alone. All other *Amici* differed! Friends in the old country had been tortured into submission. Fascista Mussolini's philosophy, is the State is first. Individual freedoms are of no importance. *Paesani* in the old country had been disciplined into submission by excruciating Castor oil management for simply suggesting freedom. Castor oil treatment subjugated *Cristiani*. Their only alternative was to sit in 50 gallon barrels which were cut in half and filled with water to defecate themselves almost to death.

Articles supposedly read in the daily I*L Progresso* Italian newspaper were argued daily by *Amici* in their own distinct dialects. Manoforte, Squagliacum, Panzanillo were all *paesani* from Frosolone, Abruzzi and nearby hamlets. Sarto was from Calabria; Un'occhio came from Sicilia; Filomena Bue left San Fele, in the region of Basilicata. Peppino was also Abruzzese coming from the Slav Italian village of Acqueviva Colle Croce. All of the *Amici* were from the poor *Mezzogiorno*, southern part of Italy.

Many times the Amici, *coversano tra di loro* (conversed among themselves) as to why and how they came to Lamerica.

They all agreed, *la miseria* (dire poverty) in Italy caused by earthquakes, drought, illnesses, high tariffs, landslides, plant lice phyelovera, lack of work and repression by land owners toward their share croppers all contributed to *morte de fame* (dying of hunger).

Relatives in America sent money to their *Famiglie* in the old country so they could travel across the sea. The purgatorial trip cost a minimum of 15.00 dollars in steerage class and took from 10 days to 2 weeks to arrive at Ellis Island. Steerage compartment located next to the ship's steering mechanism was noisy, below deck, had no port holes, dark, gloomy, crowded with three tiered bunk beds and urine odors due to a lack of toilet facilities. Men and women were separated with vertical blankets hung from ropes. Inadequate food consisted mostly of dried herring fish bought by ship owners for pennies. Passengers lost weight. Illness and death occurred.

Continuing their discussion, they talked about Italian migrants looking forward to their arrival at Ellis Island with ambivalent feelings of joy and fear. If all went well they would leave the island the same day of arrival. They feared receiving a chalk mark on their clothing from observing doctors. A chalk mark meant remaining on the island overnight and led to a complete physical the next day. Fears abounded. A physician might tag them with tricinosis of the eye or other disease's which unequivocally resulted in a purgatorial return to Italy.

Migrants were tutored by *paesani* to say that they had no contractual job awaiting them. Admitting this would be an immediate return to the old country. Rather, their response should be that they had no job but relatives and *paesani* would help them find work.

Sarto and Un'occio described how they sailed with small boats from *Calabria* and *Sicilia* to *Napoli* for embarkation

Manoforte, Squagliacum, Stumblucci and Panzanillo, said they walked 15 kilometers from Frosolone down an Appenine mountain to *Cantalupo*. A train was taken from *Cantalupo* to *Napoli*.

Filomena Bue said she and her husband walked for a day and a half from San Fele to *Potenza,* a 50 kilometer distance, to take a train to *Napoli.*

Gallo explained that he came to La'merica by using the Padrone system. Padrones were men who spoke Italian and American. A Padrone visited Gallo's village of *Quadri* and nearby villages of *Pizzoferrato* and *Civitaluparella.* The Padrone paid for steerage passage, and promised that a job would be waiting and found Gallo deplorable housing. Gallo explained, the padrone did not do this out of his kind and sympathic heart. Padrones made money by charging immigrants abnormally high interest rates. From employers they also received payment for bringing in employees. Gallo remained in New York City for more then one year to pay off his debt to the greedy Padrone. It was after debt payment that Gallo came to Buffalo.

All of the Amici were in agreement that the purgatorial anxiety-ridden trip to Lamerica led them to *la rasc di Dio* (God's abundance).

Peppino, who spoke five languages, related that the migration of 25% of the Italian population between 1880 and 1920 not only benefitted the immigrants but also helped *Italia.* Decreased population in Italy improved the economic conditions of the people that remained in the old country.

5

Migrants sent home as much as 250 dollars per year plus gift packages. Packages were wrapped in white cloth taken from 50 pound empty flower bags. The cloth covering was sewed tight to prevent pilfering. Addresses were written with indelible ink. Famiglia and Paesani, requested non perishable food products, like coffee beans and cans of tuna fish. Also sent, as asked for were shoes and long woolen underwear. By 1920, more than 700 million dollars was sent back to relatives and paisani.

Amici discussed that upon their arrival they took jobs that no one else wanted and for less pay. Jobs they accepted were ditch diggers, railroad workers, stone cutters, tunnel diggers, hod carriers and, other, poor paying jobs. They willingly put up with prejudicial insults including being called dagoes and wops as long as they could provide for LaFamiglia.

Peppino, Sarto, and Stumblucci could read and write Italian. Peppino was also literate in English and other languages. Other *Amici* waited to hear newspaper reports which were memorized. No one confronted the *inalfabeti*, (illiterates) for this would be dishonorable——anyway, illiteracy was caused by the *bestia padroni* (beast owners) who never allowed their sharecroppers to attend school. The god dammed Italian government did not give much energy to creating schools for the *contadini* (peasants). *Ricchi Uaglioni*, (rich kids) went to school, not poor children.

One of the most intense habitual arguments referenced dreams and how they translated into playing Italian numbers for a particular day. Un'occhio, the one eyed bookie, came to the shop every day to collect bets and infrequently returned to pay winners. He prayed and wished for many winners. Winning numbers, consisted of the last three bond numbers found in the business stock section of Il Progresso and American newspapers.

Peppino was a good listener. On occasion he spoke. *Amici* (friends) were intent on listening to him. The shoemaker had wisdom, knowledge, and logic to analyze the core of any problem.

Peppino ordinarily stood up front, adjacent to a full walled window pane, giving light for his shoe work.

He could see and wave to people who passed his store on Swan Street or view *Cristiani* as they turned left by Manganos Bakery onto Chestnut Street. Peppino was constantly tapping tacks, sewing, sticking, cutting, shaving, grinding, buffing, shining leather on his Landis and Mc Kay shoemaker machines. The Landis machine had strap pulleys that could be engaged to rotate the required tool. Against the wall, where Peppino

7

worked, the 13 foot long Londis machine extended half the length of the shop. The Mc Kay stitching machine was black, powerful, and used to stitch leather patches and soles on shoes. A Singer Sewing Machine, another machine in Peppino's shop, was used for lighter leather work. The shop smelled of clean, fresh leather, intermingled with the odor of adhesive glue. Adhesive glue stretched like taffy if it dripped, or if a sole had to be pulled off and realigned.

A diamond shaped, vertical metal grill was on top of the counter. Shoes were hung on the grill. The shoulder high grill permitted Peppino to see and listen to the *Amici* talking and interacting with each other. Customers walked down to the end of the counter, which was open and free of the diamond grill where business was transacted.

Peppino parted his wavy black, close-cropped hair from right to left rather than the common left to right. Short in stature with well defined

8

strong, muscled, facial jaws, black olive colored eyes and a straight nose were other physical attributes that defined Peppino as being easy on the eyes, especially when he smiled. He looked into the eyes of people. A look that was neither competitive nor intimidating, rather totally accepting. Peppino was congenial to all of his customers. Noticeably, his eyes were softer when he served *signore* and *signorine*.

On the back wall hung a picture of the Ship Rex. A ship which carried many Italians to "La Merica." Next to the Rex, hung a picture of St Theresa Avila, the patron saint of Peppino. On the wall opposite the Landis machine, hung a mirror. Below it was a Victorian couch. Four hard back chairs of different denominations were distributed in the store. A bell hung on the center entrance door. The bell rang when people entered or exited Peppino's shop. To the left, when facing the front door, was a deep window shelf filled with dilapidated ferns, jade and begonia plants that once bloomed but now had faded, creating dried up flowers and leaves that scattered all over the shelf.

An Oleander bush from Italy blossomed pink flowers. Peppino explained that the poison tea Socrates drank was made from a species of the Oleander bush. A fig tree planted in a large terra cotta pot smelled like

9

kitty litter. Finally, it was removed from the window shelf and given to Squagliacum for his backyard garden. Every fall, Squagliacum wrapped and tightened rope around the malleable fig tree branches. To lower the branches he placed a 50 gallon barrel cut in half on top. Proceeding, he filled the half barrel with water. The weight lowered the branches to the ground. This allowed him to cover the bent tree with dirt, which prevented winter freezing of the fig tree. Figs were shared with *Amici* twice a year. *Colombo figs* were large fruit sparse in number, picked in June. September brought out many juicy sweet vanilla colored, smaller figs.

The shop closed daily for lunch which lasted about an hour. Everyday, Peppino stopped and visited with his handicapped, wheel chaired, long time friend Mr. Georgio. Mr. Georgio eagerly awaited a fingertip cheek caress, a carob stick, and Peppino's soft, compassionate, encouraging voice.

Chapter 2

Strong Hands Mason Manoforte

Manoforte Martelli always volunteered to bartend the beer stand at St. Lucy's lawn fete.

Monoforte --->

Manoforte assisted Father Farelli with projects at the church even though he never attended Mass. During the week Manoforte visited the empty church. Father had callouses all over his hands caused by the manual work he did for the parish. Callouses gained Manoforte's respect. He remembered that in Italy, Priests had others do hard manual work. Parishoners not only noticed Father callouses, but also his red headed young streamlined housekeeper, Miss Kelly. She was the only Irish, red headed women in the neighborhood. In fact, parishioners didn't know any other Irish women. There were none in the neighborhood. Rumors persisted, *sotto voce*, (whispers) about Father Farelli and Miss Kelly. Manoforte was never concerned by the gossip. He held to his philosophy *"vivi e fai vivere"* (live and let live).

Manoforte made his own beer cooler expressly for the lawn fete and for other neighborhood *festa*. Into a used, 25 gallon, metal barrel was inserted a copper coil from bottom to top. Actually the coil was three times the length of rented commercial beer coolers. Hinges were welded, so the top could be closed and locked. A hole was drilled on top allowing a tapping rod to protrude. A professional saloon spigot was bolted through the silver painted, metal barrel and screwed permanently on to the coil. The tapping rod was inserted into the beer keg, pushing the cork down, and tightly bolted. A hose extending from the rod was screwed onto the bottom of the coil. A hand tire pump, attached to the rod, pressurized the keg so beer could flow through the coils. When filled in and around the coil with crushed ice, the flowing beer was colder then saloon beer.

Manoforte was a stone mason by profession. His callused hands were powerful, as was his physique. Manoforte was short with broad shoulders, straight trim vertical mid section, massively muscled forearms, and the circumference of his fingers were larger than a quarter. His straight wide nose, squared face, brown eyes, black curly hair can describe Manoforte as a handsome powerful man.

He learned his trade in Italy, as he assisted master stone masons building homes and roads. Starting work at the age of eight meant that he never attended school; he was *inalfabeti* (illiterate). Francesco his older brother, lived in the U.S. Eventually, Francesco saved sufficient money to pay for his younger brother's migration to this *bel paese,*(beautiful town).

Francesco In Italy before arriving in Buffalo, NY

At the age of nineteen Manoforte left the hamlet of Collecarrise, town of Frosolone, Abruzzi arriving in the U.S. with $35.00 in his pocket. He left Naples on the ship "San Giovanni" in steerage class, and arrived at Ellis Island on August 1, 1913. From New York City he traveled by train to Buffalo, New York to live with Francesco at 335 Seneca Street. Their planning was that Manoforte would attend school while Francesco continued working at the Erie Railroad. A week later a horrible *disgrazia* (catastrophe) struck. Francesco was crushed and died when two box cars rolled over him.

Francesco was a member of the Abruzzese Mutual Aid Self Help Society. He paid sixty cents per month for this group insurance. Societies helped when their was illness, for burial and short term loans during hardships. Actually, the Buffalo Abruzzese Mutual Aid Society was one of 887 chapters in the Sons of Italy; founded in New York City in 1905.

Grieving Manoforte left Seneca Street, and moved in as a boarder with paesano Panzanillo. The Erie Rail road hired Manoforte. He worked until he was drafted into the U.S. Army. Because of his strength he carried two fifty pound *zaino*. (backpacks). Manoforte carried his backpack and one belongings to Arturo a skinny 115 pound barber by trade. Arturo could not carry his back pack on long marches. Manoforte was asked by the drill

sergeant, if he would assist Arturo. This was

done.

The first world war came to an end when

he arrived in France. Automatically making

Manoforte a U.S. citizen because he served in the

army.

Returning to Buffalo after his honorable discharge, he worked for

other stone masons. In time, he developed private contracts leading to the

establishment of his own business.

In 1922, Signorina Lucia Martelli, no relative of Manoforte, arrived

from Acqueviva, Frosolone, Abruzzi. Though they lived within a kilometer

from each other, they were never acquainted in Italy. To come to America,

she assumed the name and credentials of her dead sister. The *consigliere*

(counselor) of Acqueviva, Signor Calasessano, encouraged Lucia to

take on her sister's identity. Lucia's *buon' anima* (good soul) sister was

eligible, within the quota limits, to come to the U.S. Lucia did not have the

credentials. Lucia migrated and moved in with Squagliacum and his wife

Dolorata, former Acqueviva neighbors.

Manoforte soon met Lucia. They were married within a year. Delorata, always chaperoned them during their courtship.

For a couple of years, Manoforte and Lucia rented a flat on Myrtle Avenue, a few doors away from the firehouse Pumper Engine #12. Lucia could read and write Italian. Her husband, Manoforte worked hard and earned money. Meticulously, Lucia saved money by walking downtown to regularly deposit funds in the Erie County Saving Bank. Mrs Amatusio a well educated women translated for customers of the bank. From the bank, Lucia continued her walk to Iroquois Gas Company and Niagara Mohawk Electric Company to pay the gas and electric bills.

Lucia learned to read and write by washing and ironing clothes for a teacher in Acqueviva. In return for washing clothes Lucia received tutored lessons.

Eventually, they bought a single, brick, two story house on Swan Street, in between the residences of Sarto and Gino Stumblucci. Immediately, Manoforte converted the previous German owned single into a double. The upper floor had one bedroom and an alcove, which served as a small bedroom. The lower floor had one bedroom. Manoforte added a concrete block addition to the back of the house, creating two more bedrooms.

Lucia, after miscarrying six children, bore a son at home delivered by a midwife. Angelo was two months premature, arriving with no finger nails and weighing three and a half pounds. A cotton filled shoe box served as a crib.

Neighbors came in, cooked meals, cleaned, made beds and washed clothes while Lucia recovered. This was the norm. When there was illness or other family problems, neighbors always helped.

As he grew, Angelo used one of the rear bedrooms. The other rooms served boarders.

← Angelo aged 2

Lucia was very protective of her son, Angelo, fearing another child loss. Manoforte was permissive, letting his son do whatever he wished. Angelo was "*orgoglioso della sua famiglia*" (pride of his family), and was loved by the boarders. Angelo spent a lot of time with his father, being partners when playing Briscola and together on woodchuck hunting trips. They were *migliori amici* (best friends).

Shoeshining

Angelo got his bootblack license when he was thirteen. Many boys tacked their licenses to homemade shoeshine boxes. A license would be revoked if Mr. Banes, childhood work inspector, caught a boy shining shoes after 6:00 pm. Word spread like *fulmine* (lightning) insuring that all the boys followed the rules when Mr. Banes was in the area.

Angelo was an enterprising, skilled innovator with his shoe shine trade. Boys had their own territories which they respected by other shiners. Angelo had two territories. One in front of the Palace Burlesque Theater during the day, the other, after 6:00 pm, against the rules, was walking from night club to night club on Seneca Street from Michigan Avenue to Main street. Luckily Mr. Banes never apprehended Angelo.

Angelo never determined why men preferred getting their shoes shined before entering the burlesque. Obviously, strippers couldn't see their feet. Well? —————— maybe later on special occasions.

Angelo's sales pitch was "How about a first class Boston gloss shine in three minutes or you won't have to pay". Above the Erie Count Bank at

Shelton Square, across from the Palace Burlesque, was a huge clock that could easily be seen. It served as a three minute timer device.

At the completion of a shine, Angelo put a penny size drop of white liquid on the toe of the shoe, and proceeded to rag it into a glistening effect. This was dramatic and different, and created many tips. Little did customers know that spit would give the same gloss, but would appear vulgar and result in no tips.

After 6:00 pm Angelo went from night club to night club, except for Ryan's, a gay bar which would not permit his entrance. Sam's Hotel, Brogans, Clarks Oasis, allowed Angelo to shine shoes. One customer was all that was needed.

Shine boys snapped the rag on the right causing a click sound. Angelo developed his own personal, innovative, signature snap. He snapped the rag on the right and left sounding click and clack. Juke boxes were always playing. Angelo had taken drum lessons at PS#6 which helped him achieve an easy click clack rhythm. "You are My Sunshine" written by the Louisiana governor, Jimmy Davis, was played perpetually. Click clack alerted other customers in the bar. When luck prevailed, he was able to get eight to ten shines, a good night's pay.

Angelo's enterprising abilities were enhanced by having a white mouse in his left hand shirt pocket. The mouse crawled out of his pocket, walked around his neck, stopped at his shoulder for a moment and returned to the food in his breast pocket. Men roared! Women screamed with alarm! The white mouse escapade made for shines and money. Angelo's income was given to His mother for family use. Astonishingly, when Angelo left for college all shoeshine money that he contributed to the family was returned to him with interest.

John, Angelo's *comba*, by way of confirmation, lived in Gaines, northern Pennsylvania. Every month, John, his father Jim Pollutro, and brothers Tony and Fred made the two and a half hour trip to Buffalo. They visited Buffalo over night to be with paesani Manoforte and Lucia. Manoforte skillfully made home fries, pork chops and *insalata* (salad) when they arrived. Manoforte, preparing for his *paesani*, had already made *pasta di casa tagliatelle* (home made long strands of 1/8 inch wide pasta). He mixed semolina flour, eggs, a small amount of water as needed and a pinch of salt; then it was mixed by hand into a ball. On a floured wooden board, he rolled out the ball of dough with a round, home made wooden, three foot long pole. It was rolled out until the dough was the thickness of a dime.

Then he proceeded to overlap the flat dough by half, then over lapped again into quarters, making sure to sprinkle flour in between layers, preventing the pasta from sticking together. Manoforte took a sharp knife in his right hand. Using his left calloused palm down hand as a guide on the sheets of pasta, he proceeded to cut 1/8 inch wide strips. When completed he placed the cut pasta in a box, separating layers with sprinkled flour and wax paper. Unbelievably the pasta was cut with minute accuracy, so it was not distinguishable from store bought linguine. Without question, Manoforte's *pasta di casa tagliatelle* shamed commercial macaroni. Paesani from Pennsylvania participated with Sunday dinners.

The sauce was made on Sunday morning with home canned tomatoes. At harvest time tomatoes were cut, and put in a *muttillo* (funnel) on top of a bottle. Tomatoes were pushed into the bottle with a round wooden stick in an up an down motion. Basil was put in the neck of the bottle. Bottle caps corked the bottle with a pressing machine, and the bottles were boiled in water to prevent spoilage.

In a pot with the canned tomatoes were added spare ribs, already fried meatballs, basil, salt and baking soda to remove tomato acidity. The *ragu* (sauce) simmered for two hours or more until the sauce became thick and *saporito* (delicious). The aroma filled the house, stimulating appetites.

The smell of Manoforte's house odor was not different than the odor emanating from other houses. The *ragu*'s blissfully ubiquitous odor simmered in the neighborhood on Sunday mornings, and Tuesday and Thursday afternoons.

Dipping bread into the sauce was common, under the guise of testing the readiness of the sauce. *Brasciole* (stuffed rolled steak) was sometimes added, then sliced and eaten along with the meatballs and ribs.

A separate pot, with salted water boiling, was made ready for the homemade pasta. A little oil added to the water prevented the pasta from sticking together. Imagine sitting at a table eating home made pasta, sprinkled with parmigiano cheese, meatballs, ribs, brasciole, stupendous delectable sauce, crusty bread, Zifandell, *vino di casa* (house wine) and being surrounded with *famiglia, paesani, amici,* telling stories, and laughing.

Salad preceded and reinvigorated appetites. It was made with tomatoes, romano lettuce arugula, vinegar (wine gone bad) and extra virgin green caste olive oil. Dessert followed. Fruit, nuts, cannoli, espresso coffee with anisetta. When fresh peaches were available, they were sliced and seeped in wine. The meals went on for at least two hours or longer.

Afterwards, the men played cards, *briscola*. Women washed dishes, discussing their children, and occasionally, problems they were having. Support and advice was shared. It was, in essence, self help therapy, only superceded by Father Farelli's advice, and his granting absolution in the confessional.

Angelo's Schooling

Angelo received a radio active crystal set with cat whiskers and ear phones from his *comba,* John. This allowed Angelo to receive a one station reception. This sparked an interest in electricity, especially building and maintaining radios. Seneca Vocational taught this. What Angelo never understood is that many of his high school classmates, non Italians, anxiously waited to be 18 years of age so that they legally could go to bars and drink. Italian neighborhood children drank wine mixed with water from the time they could drink from a glass. Reaching his junior year, Angelo decided he wanted to go to college, forgetting his previous interest in electricity, radio building and repairing.

The Turnverein an international gymnastic organization of German origin, is where Angelo met many gym teachers. Learning that 80% of the physical education teachers in Western New York attended "The Normal College of the American Gymnastic Union" located in Indianapolis, and was affiliated with Indiana University. Angelo received two years of education in the college of 80 students. The final two years were on the main campus in Bloomington, Indiana.

Angelo was a fair gymnast, a poor athlete, and a superior, natural dancer. Normal College taught all forms of dancing, folk, modern and ballroom as part of its curricula. Teaching came easily to Angelo. He could logically break down the teaching process, simplifying student learning.

In his junior year at college Angelo decided he wanted to work with families, no longer being interested in teaching physical education.

Indiana University sent the names of honor students to home town newspapers with copies mailed to parents. Proudly, Manoforte brought Angelo's honor role listing to Peppino's. Dutifully Peppino hung them on the wall. In his senior year, Angelo mailed home a copy of the Indiana University Daily Newspaper. On the front page appeared a picture of Angelo and his partner, Marolyn Mormon. In bold print, it was announced that they had spectacularly won a jitterbug contest. The picture hung in a frame on Peppino's wall. Peppino and amici awaited Angelo's letter explaining how the contest was won.

Manoforte and Lucia received Angelo's letter. The next day Manoforte took Angelo's letter to Peppino's shoe shop. Squagliacum, Panzanillo, Un'occhio Sarto and of course Peppino, who stopped work, all waited to hear the *fatto* (story). Filomena Bue arrived a little later. She first had to complete her wine sales for the day. *Siamo pronti, acconta la storia* (we are ready, recount the story). Angelo's letter, in Abruzzo dialect described the dance contest, however, jitterbug dance steps could only be recounted in English. He gave a brief history before describing the contest.

Both he and his partner, Marolyn, nicknamed "Shorty", were physical education majors. Basket weaver townees were derogatory phrases verbalized to describe physical education majors. Shorty, as noted, was short and wide hipped with a pock marked, blemished face. Status wise, basket weaver townees were the most chided and disrespected students on the Indiana University Campus.

The "organized", as the Greek Sororities and Fraternities, were called represented themselves as being the most intelligent, sophisticated,

25

distinguished group of students. Townees were students renting rooms from Bloomington homeowners. "Organized" men were easily identified. They wore yellow, pinstriped cord pants. The Women wore yellow pinstriped, wide skirts. Both genders wore black and white buck shoes. In warm weather they wore white Tee shirts with Greek logos printed on the left front pocket and on the back. In cool weather, the "organized "wore white colored sweaters and jackets with Greek embossed logos, distinguishing their individual sororities and fraternities.

Another group of students from New York, New Jersey, and Hamtramick suburb of Detroit wore draped pants, wide at the knee and narrowed to the ankle. Angelo wore drapes

Angelo's letter continued explaining the contest in dialect Italian, saying, that the night before the jitterbug contest Angelo tutored fellow students about the digestive system. He had the system completely mastered. Students were having a physiology exam on the day of the contest. Dr. Nertenberger was a Phd. physiologist in the medical school. Her difficult class was never graded on a curve. Dr. Nertenberger was very strict, except for football players who she personally tutored, insuring that they passed, or they could not play varsity. She was at every game even when the team was on the road, cheering on her tutored players.

It was not well known by the organized snobs that physical education majors were required to take science courses in the medical school. Human anatomy using cadavers, chemistry, physiology, physiology of exercise, and kineseology were all necessary for graduation. Three of Angelo's fellow students had applied and were accepted to medical schools. He had applied to the Jesuit University of St. Louis, and was accepted in the graduate school of Social Work. Dean Dr. Matte offered Angelo a full scholarship with stipends in the Indiana University PHD physical education program. This generous offer was made because Angelo finished first in his class of men and had received the Phi Beta Epsilon key award from the professional national organization of physical educators.

Angelo's letter continued, the Amici kept cheering *Bravissimo! Bravissimo!* His illiterate father, Manoforte, swelled with pride. Anxiously with the suspense building the men and Signora Bue waited to hear the description of the contest.

Continuing, the letter explained, when Angelo took the exam on the digestive system, he completely blocked and could not remember the details he had taught his classmates the previous night. Classmates and Angelo walked out of the amphitheater classroom proceeding to the university commons Rhythm Room. His introspective mood was dejection and anger toward himself for having done so poorly on the exam. Classmates encouraged, plodded, pleaded that he enter the contest with his partner, Shorty. It was of no avail! He just didn't feel like dancing.

Within the Rhythm Room a small physical education group sat in a cluster at the upper end of the room. At the other end, completely filling the long room, chattering and laughing were the yellow, pinstriped buck shoe organized. They were unmistakenly, incontrovertibly arrogantly assured that one of their own would easily win the contest. Seven organized couples were on the floor. Then it happened! The leader of the organized was prig, Jackton. His picture and articles about him appeared in every school newspaper. Tall, thin, he swaggered on the floor, displaying his presumptuousness with his tall, blond, beautiful partner. Cheered on by his pals, he was assured that he would have no competition in the contest.

Angelo's self anger switched to revenge. He told Shorty, let's dance. The small group of physical education majors smiled with happiness. Shorty and he would represent "the dumb, townee basket weavers".

Shorty and Angelo had given shows for the elderly; also put on shows in elementary and high schools. They were introduced as Short and Shorty when they were in shows. Angelo wore a zoot suit in these presentations, but obviously not in this contest, just draped pants. Shorty wore tights, anticipating she would dance.

As the contest began to the music of Count Basie's "One O'clock Jump". Shorty and Angelo performed what they considered average steps.

A referee approached them whispering "take it easy, you are frightening off the other dancers". Six couples got off the floor. The only one remaining was the Jackton tall, thin, organized couple. Now Short and Shorty let loose.

Shorty was a good athlete especially as a diver. A one and half somersault on a low board was a simple dive for her.

Angelo pushed his open right hand against Shorty's open right hand. She twirled three time on one foot. Reversing this Shorty pushed Angelo's right hand into a triple twirl on one foot. They broke a number of times, creating distant from each other coming together performing the Camel Walk, Shorty George, Chicken Hop and Cass Daily. Angelo did rubber knees while Shorty encircled him. They both tap danced the time and sand step with arms outstretched to the side, palms and foreheads touching. Keeping their heads touching they turned themselves gracefully around and around. He threw Shorty over his left shoulder as his legs were slightly bent at the knees. She twirled and did a full split. Shorty led, so they were back to back with uplifted arms. She bent forward, pulled and rolled Angelo over her back into a full split. By this time, the Jackton couple walked off the floor trounced and disgraced in defeat! The final move of the routine was the windmill step. Shorty's back was toward Angelo. He lifted her as She straddled her legs around his waist as he rotated around and around. Surprisingly the organized clapped, whistled, stomped their feet, shouting "Great! Great! Great! impossible to do"! They were cheering for Short and Shorty not for their own organized couple. Physical educator classmates lifted their chests. Angelo and Carolyn were applauded back for a number of encores.

A few days later, Angelo received his physiology digestive system

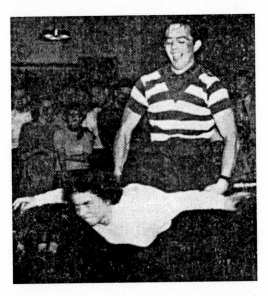

grade back, receiving an unaccustomed C+, rather than the usual A. Dr.

Mertenberger stapled a picture of the windmill step which appeared on the

front page of the "Daily Student Newspaper" taken by student photographer,

Bill Mallen. A note said "Next time think physiology not jitterbugging".

"Bravissimo! Bravissimo! Angelo "broughta *orgoglu* (pride) to

da Italiani fora doing a gooda ata da universida, anda da *vittoria* ofa da

contesta froma da Medegons". The framed windmill jitterbug dance step

picture hung on Peppino's wall for years.

Chapter 3

Panzanillo Polo and the Pull Chain Toilet

Francesco, Manoforte's brother, died within a week of his arrival from Italy. As a result, Manoforte did not wish to grieve alone so he moved in as a border with his *paesano*, the Panzanillo (little belly) family. There were four borders in the three bedroom flat, including Stella, Panzanillo's wife and their three male children. Luckily, the boarders worked three shifts.

The one bed slept one or two borders at a time.

Panzanillo was a bookie by profession. He supported his family as a bookie plus the income from the boarders. Two of his sons copied their father's example and eventually became bookies, after finishing the eighth grade at PS#6.

Panzanillo migrated from Frosolone, Campobasso, Italy. He was an expert with numbers and odds, disregarding his being *inalfabet* (illiterate). The *abitanti* (population) of Frosolone was 5,900 people when he migrated to Buffalo, NY.

Frosolne was well known all over Italy, for their *artigiani* (craftsman) who made knives, swords, scissors. The *artigiani* speculated that their craft arose when the Roman legions came through the Apennines, needing cutlery. The Frosolonesi made them, resulting in their becoming expert craftsman. Historically, this may or may not be true. It is however, a pleasing fable which doesn't deny the expertise of Frosolonesi in making swords, various specimen of knives, sartorial and other types of scissors.

Panzanillo (little belly) was endeared to Marco Polo. He heard many adventurous Polo stories as told by the townspeople. His respect of Marco was actualized by naming one of his children Polo. The family of little belly lived in a six family brick building owned and rented out by absentee

landlady, Mrs. Doyle. She lived in a mansion, which was no surprise, in an

exclusive neighborhood on Delaware Avenue. Next door to the six flat brick

building stood in all its glory, Scimmias Saloon, nicknamed the Monkey

House. From Italian to English *scimmia* translates into monkey. In the rear

of Doyle's apartment building was a lumber yard. A 12 foot high rough

hewn oak fence separated Doyle's property from the lumber yard.

At the moment this doesn't seem out of the ordinary, however a major

problem existed. The tenants in Doyle's building all ate at approximately

5:00 o'clock, after husbands returned from work. Now, it can easily be

appreciated that the gastro colic reflex originated with many of the tenants

 at the same time. Meaning that long lines waited to get into

the *baccausa* which happened to be a luxury. The inside toilet

was not a "two holer" with a Sears and Roebuck catalog for

viewing and wiping. In fact, it was a Victorian pull chain toilet

with a five gallon porcelain closet near the ceiling. Children

could easily reach a porcelain knob at the end of a long brass

chain to make flushes. The toilet itself had a wooden, oak seat.

All of these ingredients was considered the latest in modern technological design and function. This pull chain served six families, numbering 41 people plus many visiting guests who described *quant e bell quil baccaus*, (what a beautiful toilet). Considering these conditions, Gino Stumblucci, the neighborhood, self learned plumber made frequent visits to use and repair Mrs. Doyle's pull chain toilet.

Polo decided he was not going to wait in line. He was in a hurry to go out and play kick the can with his friends. His ingenious plan would prove to be calamitous. Walking to the back of the building, he opened a first floor window, pulled down his pants, put his ass out on the window sill, sitting comfortably to deficate. Cataclysmic disaster happened! Polo slipped and fell out of the window. His "U" positioned body, feet and head up, ass down, was ensnared between the slivered fence and the brick building. If he remained quiet, he did not descend, but he realized that he could not stay in this position, with his pants over his ankles, his ass down for the rest of his life. Any way he had to go play kick the can with his buddies.

He hollered "Help!" in English. *"Aiutami! Aiutami!"* in Italian. The more he screamed, the more he sank further down, encouraging slivers to slide into his ass. Polo kept hollering, descending lower, multiplying slivers. His "U" shaped, slivered, bare body reached the bottom of the fence.

Crying and sobbing he continued to scream in English and Italian "Help!",

"*Aiutami!*"

Lily, a teenager heard the noise and screams as she passed the window. She looked out the window. She laughed as she saw Polo at the bottom of the fence. Pants at his ankles, bare naked to his waist. Realizing the graveness, Lily hurried to tell those in line toilet tenants of Polo's dire circumstance. They all ran and peeked down from the window. Laughing, they ran to the lumber yard to report the *disgrazia* (disaster).

Manoforte, with the lumber yard workers, easily found where Polo was lodged by hearing his cursing and swearing. "Sonovabitch, bastard" he said, crying and sobbing. Manoforte, pulled and removed two eight inch wide planks with his strong, bare, calloused hands, disregarding the crow bars brought by the lumber yard workers.

Sensitively, Manoforte cradled Polo in his arms and ran to Emergency Hospital, on the corner of Clinton and Pine Streets, six blocks away. Three doctors and four nurses spent two and a half hours removing the slivers from Polo's buttocks. From then on his nick name became Oak Ass Polo.

This *disgrazia* was always talked about at wakes and weddings. At Peppino's shop the Amici revealed their *condoglianze* (condolences) with sad faces, lifting and lowering their pointed up clumped fingers, signifying "things like this unfortunately happen". Inside, their hearts were laughing.

Another heresy happened to the Panzanillo, little belly family. It was a *segreto de la famiglia,* (family secret) but like many family confidences – it got out.

Panzanillo told Polo to get wine from the cellar. Polo went to the cellar, blessing himself before the crucifix in the wine compartment. Crucifixes prevented wines from turning into vinegar, as well as imploring *Dio* (God) to make the wine superior.

Polo put the *muttil,* funnel on top of the bottle, placed it under the copper brass spigot, and turned it on. Nothing happened? – No wine poured out! Polo ran upstairs, hollering "PaPa there is no wine"!

Panzanillo shuddered; his heart beat faster. *"Impossible, it's a newa barile"* (barrel). Panzanillo with his three boys rushed to the cellar. Stella did not join them. No wine even dripped out of the spigot. The barrel was easily moved. Obviously, no wine was in the barrel. PaPa moved to the back of the barrel. The torturous truth was made apparent. There were holes in the back from top to bottom. Holes were made to drain the wine out, inch by inch.

Stella liked to drink. Yes she made holes every day to imbibe. The crucifix was not powerful enough to prevent Stella's hole drilling wine drinking.

Preventive corrections were instantly made. The wine barrel back heads were placed against the wall, so no one including Stella could go behind to make holes. A bigger crucifix was supported with an icon of St. Morand, one of eight patron saints of wine makers. St. Morand lived for the forty days of each lent on a single bunch of grapes.

No one was to reveal the heresy. Panzanillo was always asked how Stella was feeling by the *Amici* at Peppino's. For years his friends never inquired. Why now?

Oak Ass Polo grew into manhood. He wasn't a good copier, therefore didn't follow his father and brother's bookie trade. Instead, he worked as an iron worker at the Community Steel prefabrication plant on Myrtle Avenue near South Cedar Street. Polo married Loretta, a neighborhood woman. He rented a flat across from his work place, next door to his in-laws.

Polo's Wedding

The wedding reception was held in the basement of St. Lucy's Church, starting at 5:00 in the afternoon. A kitchen and bar were at the back end of the hall. Manoforte was the bartender with his famous homemade silvercolored, beer cooler. Other drinks served were anisette, strega, sambucca made at home with alcohol bought from Filomena Bue. The alcohol was 100% when purchased and tested. A teaspoon of alcohol was lit with a match. If it was completely burned off it was considered 200 proof. Water and spirits of flavoring were added. A gallon of alcohol made 16 quarts of 50 proof liquor. Home made root beer was made for children. To a container holding five gallons of water was added 2.5 ounces of root beer extract, five pounds of sugar, plus a five pound block of dry ice. The top of the container was loosely covered allowing for bubbling pressure to escape. After 30 minutes, carbonation reached a suitable point for the root beer to be placed in bottles and capped. Red and white wine from Panzanillo's cellar had no ending.

St. Lucy's hall had four inch diameter pipes down the center to hold the church floor up. Dancing took place by avoiding the poles. This was easily accomplished except for the Tarantella, which required skill to avoid bouncing against the poles. A stage for musicians was at the front end of the hall. Squagliacum's son, Umberto, played the trumpet. Eugenio, the son-in-law of Squagliacum, was a piano player. Eugenio, as well as the other musicians, could play any standard tunes from illegal fake books which listed chords, melodies and words.

 Sheet music gave royalties to composers, fake books costing $20.00 did not. Eugenio, in time memorized the entire fake book, meaning more the 100 standards. Songs not listed in the book were hummed to Eugenio. His brilliant ear easily memorized the hummed melody. Sarto's son Carlo played drums. Filomena Bue had a multi-talented son Vito who played classical guitar. When he played classical, he held the base of the instrument in his lap. Playing jazz and standards he held the curvature of the guitar on his right thigh. Vito was adept with any string instrument including the mandolin, which was notable when he sat in with the Italian, immigrant, playing musicians. Bertho,

Peppino's son, played tenor sax and was also the singer in the combo, called the "High Tones." Young people danced to standards: "Body and Soul" "I Surrender Dear" "Don't Take Your Love From Me" "Pennies from Heaven"

requesting that "Stardust" be played frequently. "Good Night Sweetheart" ended the gig. During the High Tones break, Squaliacum played the *organetto*, accompanied by Vito's mandolin with half assed guitar cording of Vito's mother Filomena Bue.

Parents and their children danced to Italian songs. *"La Mazzuca di Carolina," "Torna a Sorrento," "O Marie," "O Mama," "Parlami d'Amore Mari," "Chitarra Romana," "Una Boce Da More," "Tesoro Mio,"* and naturally without failure the Neopolitan and Sicilian Tarantella. Almost everyone in the hall, including young children joined in the Tarantella dancing around the four inch pipes.

Squaliacum, Filomena Bue, Vito and the High Tones all joined together playing the Tarantella. Expert Tarantella dancers stepped into the center of the circular dancers showing off inventive skilled steps, holding and twirling partners, left and right arms locked at the elbows. Other's clapped their hands under raised legs, then twirled individually with their fingers snapping above their head. Borrowed tambourine from Carlo, the drummer, kept time by alternated banging the tambourine on the thigh, then over head hitting it with their free hand. Perspiration resulted because of these athletic movements.

Legends of the tarantella abound. The dance is sometimes referred to as the spider dance, meaning that a person, mostly women, bitten by the tarantella, begin moving and jumping into frenzied dancing to end the pain, and this caused a cure.

Another legend describes the Tarantella as a courtship dance. The male's dancing steps and body movements expressed his love for his partner.

The evening was spent drinking and eating peanuts. Shells were thrown on the, varnished, wooden floor. Slippery shelled floors necessitated balanced dancing. Falls seldom happened.

Bread, in large round loaves, were baked in Mangano's wood burning, brick ovens. Each baked loaf cost five cents. The bigger the loaf the cheaper the cost. Signor Mangano checked if the loaves were cooked by slipping his longhandled, wooden, shovel tool under the loaf bringing them to the entrance of the oven to determine if they were baked. When completed, he shoveled under the sesame colored light brown, hot loaves pulling them out, and placing them in Signora's towels to be carried home.

For the wedding 24 huge loaves of bread and 14 bushels of cookies were made. Sarto let Panzanillo's wife Stella and bride-to-be Loretta, use his fullsized pizza, oven to bake the cookies prepared in advance with the help of neighbors. *Pizzelle* were baked with an olive oiled sprinkled cast iron machine, placed over an open gas flame. Cookies were Sicilian *cucidati, biscotti* with anise and almonds, *mustaccioli, gugilini, sfinge, pinulata, pasticciotti, cannoli* and *taralli*, boiled before being baked.

Polo and his *bride* Loretta departed the hall, with out anyone knowing, at 7:30. They walked from St. Lucy's church hall down Chicago Street for one block, turned left at Myrtle Avenue to their rented flat. While, Loretta and Polo were walking neigbors shouted from their windows and porches.

Auguri! Auguri! Auguri! (best wishes) friends were throwing *confetti* (candy covered almonds) not rice. Children followed them to pick up and eat the *confetti*.

Polo took off his tuxedo borrowed from Sottaterra the funeral director. Loretta's long white, satin gown, made by Filomena Bue, was put in a box to be returned, to be used by the next neighborhood bride.

In front of the house, Umberto's, $34.50 car was parked. The car had no top. They prayed that it would not rain during the two hour drive to Niagara Falls for their three day honeymoon. Loretta made sure she brought the saltshaker her mother gave her. Her mother insisted that the nuptial bed be sprinkled with salt, insuring that pregnancies and grandchildren would arrive soon, but not before nine months.

As the evening came to a close, sandwiches wrapped in wax paper were passed out. Caciocavallo, peppers and onion *frittatas*, salami and most prized but limited capocolla sandwiches. Two salami were traded for one capocolla sandwich. Children tossed sandwiches, trading with each other. Wax paper covering was necessary to prevent olive oil, salami and Capocolla fats from leaking over clothes or mixing with the peanut shells making for a dangerous, slippery floor.

Espresso coffee made with ten borrowed Neopalitan Macchinetta, was accompanied with cookies and served as *dolce* (dessert).

Father Farella and his red headed, shapely, Irish housekeeper, Miss Kelly, were always invited to wedding receptions. Finally, Father Farella clicked the lights off signifying the evening was to end. The six a.m. Mass was to start in three hours. Miss Kelly and Father hadn't been to bed yet. An Italian songfest accompanied by Squagliacum's Organetto continued in the streets. Many joined in singing *"Mazzolini di Fiori," "O Sole Mio," "Santa Lucia," "La Molisana," "Torna A Sorrento." "O Mamma," "Un Bacio d'amore,"* and *"Vicin U Mare."* It is doubtful that any of the wedding guests went to Mass. They stayed home sleeping off wine and capocolla sandwiches.

It became obvious that salt sprinkled on the nuptial bed didn't guarantee children. Everyone in the neighborhood gossiped about Loretta not getting pregnant. Was their something wrong with Polo? He looked *forte* (strong) and eager. The women in the neighborhood blamed him. Men on the other hand said maybe Loretta was like an "ica boxa". Dr. Meranti, the dentist, regular doctors cost too much money, advised Polo to go home for lunch. This would certainly help toward Loretta's getting pregnant. After three months, Polo was tired. Three time's a day, morning, lunch hour and at night, still nothing happened. Only one other alternative remained. Loretta and Polo made special Novenas. At St. Mary's Redemtorist Church, on Pine and Broadway they made a nine day Novena, once per week to St. Alponsus the patron saint for pregnancy.

Polo left work at 3:30 on Wednesdays, so that he

and Loretta could walk to the 4:00 Novena. He even sang

"Mother Dear Pray for Me" to strengthen prayers. Polo

and Loretta were not taking any chances, reinforcing their

Novena at St. Mary's by attending a Novena to St. Rita,

patron saint for genologic ailments. They walked two miles to St. Rita's

Church at102 Seymour Street in the midst of an Irish neighborhood which

could be dangerous. Italian and Irish gangs often fought each other, even

though both groups were Roman Catholic. St. Rita's Novena was held only

on Tuesday evenings at 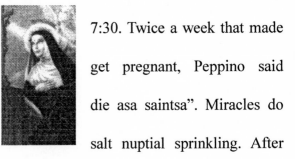 7:30. Twice a week that made

Novenas. If Loretta didn't get pregnant, Peppino said

"daya, woulda ata leasta die asa saintsa". Miracles do

happen, irregardless of the salt nuptial sprinkling. After

six double novenas Loretta was pregnant. Polo was happy. He didn't have

to go home for lunch. Fertility prospered. Within six years they had six

children. The only way they could prevent further children was to have Polo

moved into his mother-in-law's house next door. After two weeks, Loretta

and Palo decided this was not to be a continued practice. Father Farella

suggested under the dire circumstances, dire action would be necessary.

They were advised to make a special Novena to St. Jude, patron saint of lost causes. Loretta with Polo took the advice. Once again, they took the street car, but this time traveled to St. Jude's Shrine, 193 Elk Street.

St. Jude was merciful. There were no more children. Polo and Loretta could live together in the same bed.

Chapter 4

A Letter
Regarding Stumbluccis'
Disgrazia

Dear Amico Michael Giallombardo

Here I was amidst a canyon of books, high in the racks of the library of the Jesuit's at St. Louis University. As in most library stacks, it was dim, quiet, dreary with dusty floors and manuscripts.

I had just completed reading two professional articles for a graduate course in social work and was goading myself to overcome my resistance to reading the third and final article.

Lethargic and bored, I began the reading. Within a few minutes my emotional state changed from lethargy to eager inquisitiveness and total involvement. The core of the article went on to explain that many physical anomalies which are commonly thought of as being genetic in origin are in reality psycho-culturally caused. We as human beings copy the people around us. We especially model or take example from our parents. The article thoroughly defined strabismus as being, a modeled physical handicap.

The article described a litany of other such copied physical traits, including talipes varus.

My enthusiasm was high pitched. Within a few weeks I would be going home for the Thanksgiving holidays. With this new, significant knowledge I was going to miraculously cure my *paesani*, the Stumblucci family.

Following an uneventful, restless, half slept twelve hour train ride on the New York Central, I arrived in Buffalo, NY, and visited his family. The next day I visited the Stumblucci family.

At this time of year the upper east side was filled with the aroma of freshly pressed wine grapes. In front of almost every house, except where the *Medegons* lived, one could view bushels filled with varied hues of purple and golden, dried, hard caked, pressed grapes.

One could look down the parallel streets of Swan, North Division, South Division, Seneca, Eagle and hidden Myrtle Avenue and see burgundy colored bushels lined up near curbstones. Now, you must realize that there was a great deal of status connected with grape pressings. Neighborhood men appearing blase would abstrusely and critically evaluate the mashings. Teams of men pressed the grapes so tight that not even an "goccia di vino"(not a drop of wine) was left in the pressings. Actually the grapes were pressed so dry, they could be burned. They were seldom burned. Showing off the pressings with pride was preferred. Further distinction had to do with the type of grapes used. The experienced wine maker could identfy the type of wine by a mere glance of the pressing.

This was near the end of the depression 1937. A few families that could afford to do so, pooled their penny-saved money to buy California muscatel grapes from the farmers' Clinton-Bailey Market. The pressings were golden in color. Other winemakers mixed muscatel with alicanti or Zinfandel grapes to give a burgundy color to the wine.

The pressings of people on welfare or day laborers were deep, dark purple made from the homegrown, Silver Creek delivered, foxy smelling, *la brusca* concord grapes.

I walked into the back yard of the Stumblucci home. There was Mr. Gino Stumblucci threading some pipes. I addressed him with the traditional respectful Zio Gino *"Come stai* (How are you)?"

His eager reply "Angelo, How youa ara, itsa nisa to see ua backa fromna scoola. My hands isa dirty ora I shaka hands widda you."

Zio Gino was a self taught unlicenced plumber and general neighborhood handyman. His shortness of stature, allowed him to stand up and work in most cellars. Crawl spaces meant he laid on his back vis a vi Michaelangelo to repair pipes. Years of using a pick and shovel made for calloused hands. Zio spoke with a soft, hesitant, almost stammering, quiet voice. He had a few other traits that were uncommon. He always carried a rosary and always blessed himself with the sign of the cross if anyone *bestemmiava* (swore).

It was a many times told neighborhood *"fatti"* (story) that Gino was digging a sewer next to the Allhands strip tease night club, when Gino heard much hollering, swearing, blaspheming and cursing. He compulsively and repetitively started crossing himself. Further, he strengthened himself with God's graces by saying hourly rosaries. Ordinarily, a job like this only took a day and half to complete. But considering the unparalleled tribulations it took him six days "to doa da joba".

Very few people outside of his immediate family knew that Zio Stumblucci could read and write in Italian and English. Every day he would pick up a day old "Il Progresso" newspaper from Martellinoe's tobacco store. Outwardly, this was done to carry his plumbing pipes. Gino didn't want the neighborhood to know he was literate. If this was recognized, he would be writing letters to the old country for everybody on the upper East side. He would never be able to dig holes.

There was one remaining trait that did not take much attention to observe. Peppino the shoemaker, the local social commentator said that one of the reasons Gino became a plumber was that "he coulda diga and staya ina six feeta deepa holes so nobodya coulda seea hisa feeta pointing ata eacha other". Zio Stumblucci suffered from talipes varus. He was pigeon-toed.

Zia Matalena, Zio's wife, embraced me with both her arms reaching up and around my chest. It was a sincere warm reception. I didn't mind the garlicy smell of her kiss on my check. After all, the nasal senses are the first to accommodate. And next to the seasonal new wine odor prevailing throughout the neighborhood, garlic was an indigenous, always present, accepted, gastronomic, enticing smell. Good to fight the Spanish flu, *mal occhio* (evil eye), diarrhea, rheumatism, tape worms, swellings, and anything else. You can add whatever diseases or illness is wished because garlic would "cura anyteeng". Anyway, garlic made everyteeng *saporito*.

Zia Matalena, had long black hair that never was seen full length but always rolled into a bun. In fact, most neighborhood women had long hair. Inadvertently, one might see the bun unfolded revealing long glistening thick, usually black hair hanging past the waist. Stories were told. When times were hard the hair was sold to wig makers. Ordinarily, however, it was tight pulled hair against the temples, formed into a round ball, pierced by a number of ferrets, that were allowed to be seen.

Zia Matalena was shorter than her husband. An expected characteristic for neighborhood couples. She had a round face. Naturally red, wrinkled skin stretched over high cheek bones. The wrinkles were a residual of her many younger years spent shepherding animals in the windy sunny Appenine mountains of Abruzzo.

She had long hairs on her chin; kids called it a beard. Her voice, raspy and gregariously loud, was definite. This probably developed from constantly calling her five kids into the house to go to the store. This was often, because the family only had an ice box not a refrigerator. Her vocabulary was interspersed with *sonnva bitchee and bestia.*

As an aside, Zio Gino loved his wife, but was always blessing himself in her presence. Peppino wondered if Zia Matalena swore in bed.

Actually, Zia Matalena's figure, if one chose to call it a figure, resembled a rectangular box which stood upon its short base.

Any respected visitor could expect outward immediate hospitality. "Sita downa Angelo, I gota soma *acquata"* (new wine made by passing water through grape pressing), *cacio cavallo* (a form of provolone) and *pane di casa* (hot homemade bread). Before I could say anything, I was seated at the table and lavished with food.

I loved Zia Matalena, but leaving feelings aside, it becomes my responsibility to mention a very observable physical handicap. Matalena Stumblucci suffered from *occhi stuort.* She unfortunately suffered from strabismus. She was cross eyed

Zio and Zia Stumblucci had five children. Four boys and a girl. Alfredo, the oldest was tall with blond curly hair and blue eyes. A track star specializing in the 880 event. Michelino, their second, was also tall with black wavy hair, and was considered one of the best quarter milers in the city. Ernesto, their third, had red heavy strait hair and resembled his father in shortness and general stature. Like his brothers, he also was on the High School track team. Giovanella was clear skinned with black shiny eyes smiled and laughed easily. She had natural artistic talent, and was considered the best drawer in grammar school. She already had won a juvenile scholarship to attend the Albright Art Gallery.

Finally, Roberto the youngest. He was in the 6th grade at PS 6. He was the best artist in his class, got straight A's and wanted to be a track star like his brothers. The family Americanized his name and called him Babio. After all, America had to be honored. There were always cracks and innuendos in the neighborhood about how tall these kids grew from short parents and "where the hell did the blond and red head come from!" Those gossipers who were kinder and gentler said "Ita musta be dat da familas *genitori* (ancestors) coma froma alta Italia, a longa tima ago. Alla peopla is talla witta blonda hair from Norta Italia."

Others *sott voce* (whispered), "Zia Matalena musta hada a comba visating sometimes ore maybe ita wasa da newspaperman". Neighbors laughed this off. Nobody in the neighborhood had a newspaperman.

You probably realizes that I have diverted from continuing the family's descriptive appearance. It torments me to say, but must be revealed, that the Stumblucci kids were good copiers. They modeled their loving parents. They all suffered with a Disgrazia (a misfortune). Like the father, they were all pigeon-toed. And you probably guessed, like the mother, they were all cross eyed.

Zio and Zia Stumblucci did everything they could to cure the family. They had Francesca *La Lurda* (the dirty one) come into the house for a number of months on a daily basis to try her *Maluocchio* (evil eye ritual cure) on the kids and also stressed using an amulet. Water and oil was used as part of the exhortations. After using two gallons of

100% pure Leone olive oil imported from Italy, the family gave up.

Consistently, on a weekly basis, the family dressed in the best they had and went to *La Chiesa de Santa Lucia (St Lucy's Church)*. Zio Stumblucci, as short as he was, walked in the center flanked by tall Alfredo and Michelino. Ernesto and Babio were in the second row. Finally, in the back, as was expected, Zia Matalena and Giovanella followed. They could hardly be seen shaded by the height of the older boys.

They walked straight, attempting to give a confident appearance. Beneath this exterior, one could sense a feeling of familial embarrassment.

As they walked down Swan Street, especially during the warm summer months, the family was looked upon. Windows were wide open. Neighbors hung out of windows and talked to each other. The fresh air was a relief from the hot stuffy flats. The neighbors knew that it was Wednesday night, 6:45 p.m. How? The Stumblucci family was on their way to the

weekly novena in honor of *Santa Lucia,* the patron saint of the blind

Mothers and grandmothers would make the sign of the cross and

pray for the family as they passed. With the deepest compassion they would

utter *"Che povera familia Disgraziata"* (what an unfortunate family).

Generally, however, adults would cross the street, remain in hallways,

and use other tactics so as not to encounter the family.

To meet all of these Christians head on was a catastrophe. It was

like meeting an ancient Greek military wedge. Zio Stumblucci, Alfredo and

Michelino walking pigeon-toed toward you, but their eyes crossed toward

their father. Their father looked straight ahead but his feet pointing toward

each other. A handshake became an exasperating process. If one looked down

at the family's feet, it would be considered disrespectful and additionally,

engendered confusion. Their feet pointing toward each other, yet somehow,

someway, the family managed to walk forward.

To look them straight in the eyes, using a figure of speech, was

impossible and only caused dizziness. Rather then being exposed to this

uncomfortable nervousness, neighbors avoided them as a family and chose

to talk to the Stumblucci's on an individual basis.

Kids, however, were heartless. They would shout from windows, *"Buona sera"* (Good evening) to the family. After the Stumblucci's graciously responded, the kids would step back into the house, cup their hands over their mouth, snickered and tried to guess who was looking at who, and who was stepping where. If they got caught by their parents, they duly and justifiably were given a *calcio in cullo* (a kick in the ass) for being disrespectful. When the kids were not around, the adults followed their children's lead and hypocritically laughed at the incidents.

It was concluded by the neighborhood that Gino Stumblucci purposefully moved to the parish of *Santa Lucia.* He did this so a miricle would be performed to cure his "disgraziata" family of their affliction.

Peppino, the shoemaker, questioned if *Santa Lucia* cured the family's eyes would Gino move to the parish of St. Peregrine in Mt Vernon, New York. St. Peregrine "isa da patrona sainta of da feeta".

I sat with Zio and Zia Stumblucci and explained that I was taking a behavior modification course in school. Being a *paesano* of theirs, my parents came from the same Italian Village, I would like to cure Babio of his misfortunes. Babio was picked because he was the youngest and probably the most pliable, —- I thought?

Gino and Matalena stunned and momentarily quiet, looked at each other, in the only way they could. There was a moment of hesitancy. Zia looked at me with her crossed eyes; and eagerly accepted. "Yesa Angelo, youa gonna do wata you wanna. Aftera youa cura Babio, we gonna hava a biga festa".

The next day I started my cure.

Kitchens and dining rooms were sacredly esteemed by all the Cristiani in the neighborhood. The kitchen was the center of all family activities. Talking, sharing, teasing, hollering, shouting, breaking bread took place in the kitchen.

Dining rooms were second in distinction. Dining rooms were supposedly used only on special occasions. Sundays, holidays, birthdays, name days and birthdays of the saints. It is to be recognized that every village in Italy had their own particular patron saint. Every Christian name was adopted from a relative. Relatives adopted the names of saints. I could go on and on, but it becomes apparent that there are hundreds of combinations that can be concocted to create excuses for using the dining room. Living rooms or parlors as they were known, hardly existed. *Medegons* used parlors to eat cookies and drink weak coffee. Italians sat with their arms on the table, drank wine, ate *supresciato*, (homemade dried sausage), s*camorza* (a type of mozzarella), all of which was accompanied by eating freshly torn apart hot crispy bread.

Americans said please for everything that had to be passed and kept their arms on their laps under the table. Peppino said the "*Medegons* useda so many pleases datta no onea coulda getta fatta".

Former parlors, once used by Americans, were turned into bedrooms. Even with this additional room transformation, there was usually a minimum of three kids to a bed.

Dining rooms were large. Stumblucci's dining room was extra large. During the day a small amount of natural light came in from two side-wall windows. The light was limited because the Stumblucci house was separated only by a few feet from their next door neighbor's house.

In the center of the room was a round, extendable, dark- stained oak table. Along one side wall, was a long buffet topped with heavy marble. Hanging above the buffet, on the papered wall was a picture of Saint

Lucy. Saint Lucy was nun and held out a dish  dressed like a compulsive containing two eyes. Beneath the picture on the buffet marble top was a constantly burning votive candle. The candle flickered within a burgundy- colored, glass holder. Every neighborhood corner store had massive supplies of votive candles. Every Christiani prayed for some kind of miracle. Though, hitting the Italian lottery numbers was the miracle most petitioned.

In the center of the ceiling above the table hung a tarnished brass chandelier, The brown painted floor was covered with a blue-red large flowered linoleum. *Medegons* had wool rugs and vacuum cleaners. Their soft, white, sticky bread never spilled on the floor. Italian hard crusted sesame seed covered bread spattered all over the table and floors when torn apart. Linoleum was easily cleaned with a broom and mop.

Let me explain a common domestic custom pertaining to the cleaning of linoleum. They were washed weekly on hands and knees, proceeded by hand polishing with a slippery wax. This was followed by covering the entire floor with newspapers. When company visited, the newspapers were removed to make a "*bella figura*" (beautiful appearance). The glistening reflective floor was shown off.

I decided to use the dining room for the cure. It would be better if I kept Saint Lucy and the votive lamp on my side.

Babio was with me. My immediate task was to design a program to straighten out his eyes and feet. I came up with an ingenious scheme that would have shamed Pavlov. I would straighten Babio's eyes and feet at one and the same time.

I took two bananas from the always present fruit bowl and hung them with a string to the chandelier. One banana was hung from the left extending arm. The other was hung from the right hornlike extension. Both were hung close to the bulging, pregnant, center post.

I sat Babio at the table. He planted his right foot on the floor next to the right leg of the table, and did likewise with his left foot next to a left leg of the split, expandable table. My prescription: Babio was to exercise twice daily for one-half hour intervals. Once in tho morning before school, and later in the afternoon upon returning from classes.

Babio was to stare at the bananas and simultaneously keep his feet pointed in an outward ducklike position against the feet of the table.

Daily, we would gradually separate the bananas and likewise slowly spread apart the table. My optimistic calculations determined that within thirty days, his eyes and feet would become as straight as a Roman viaduct.

While staring at the bananas with his feet spread, he meditated on all kinds of topics. He wondered, with straight eyes and feet, if the girls in his class would like him and talk to him face to face. This fantasy inspired him to disciplined continuance of the prescription. After a week of this, "stupid miracle plan" Babio's meditation turned toward the "dumb bastard Angelo who designed the cure".

The second week, he continued due to the prodding of his mother, with a wooden spoon, and the support of his father and siblings. They encouraged him. "We can see a change already Babio". Considering the ocular distortion of the family, I wondered how they could really notice any changes. Frankly, I was beginning to doubt my ingenious treatment plan.

Finally, Babio rebelled. He gave up and skipped the exercises, preferring to help his family press the wine grapes in the cellar.

Now commenced the beginning of the end.

The family was occupied making wine. The bananas were left unsupervised. The skins developed speckles. Then the skins turned completely brown, shriveled, wrinkled, became black and finally cracked open and fell. The bananas followed a natural order and proceeded to ferment. The room smelled vinegary.

Simultaneously, as this metamorphic fermenting process was taking place, fruit flies invaded the bananas and continued to prodigiously procreate. Did they ever multiply! Within a few days, there must have been three-hundred generations of fruit flies buzzing and reproducing, all over these hanging rotting fermenting bananas.

Had Gregor Mendel walked into the Stumblucci dining room, he would have given up his study of pea pods and reverted to the use of these promiscuous fruit flies for his genetic experiments.

Giovanella, came upstairs from the cellar to get a large *muttil* which was stored in the buffet. She stepped into the darkened dining room. Yes, she stepped on the proverbial banana peel. The interaction of the banana on the newspaper which lay on the waxed slippery linoleum was like stepping on a floor covered with highly greased precision ball bearings.

Giovanella's legs gave way. With a slamming thud, she landed on her back and hollered out an imploring "Maddona help me!"

Zia Stumblucci ran upstairs with her straight legs. She did not evaluate conditions; rather impulsively plodding into the dining room. Zia Matalena was always confident that her straight legs would balance her 4' 8", 180 pound rectangular shaped body. She slipped! Her left leg flew up into the air. Her right foot continued straight ahead. She resembled King Kong without the hair, doing a tour jete leap. She tripped over Giovanella and fell full force, face forward on her daughter. Her wine stained *mandazin*, (apron) flew up. So did her black dress and black petticoat. Beneath, could be seen her long black stockings held in place by garters. A slight amount of thigh was revealed. Her legs were as round and sturdy as any pillar of the Vatican.

Covering her, enormously wide thick buttocks was a pair of homemade off-white bloomers. The inscription in the middle of her bloomers, read "Hector's Fine Flour". Below were three evenly distributed X's side by side and a band of blue encircled the red logos.

The bloomers were made from fifty- pound, flour sacks. Sacks were bleached and used for bloomers, table cloths, *mappina*, (dish cloths), towels, wash cloths, etc., etc. The La Stella neighborhood company, chlorine solution obviously did not bleach out the dyed inscriptions on the flour bag.

As she fell like a hippopotamus on Giovanella, she gave out a prodigious f a r t that resembled Vesuvius exploding. The fart was reinforced by her verbal pronunciation, *"O cazz"* (O penis)!

The rest of the family flew upstairs. Alfredo slipped in an effort to control himself, he grabbed the chandelier. For an instant, he looked like Tarzan flying through the air. The chandelier fell. Tarzan landed on his mother and sister.

Michelino and Ernesto were no more *"fortunato"*. They both flew into the air head first and multiplied the human pyramid.

Zio Gino, who was always meticulously cautious, got to the door and stopped. Peppino said later,"hea wasa saveda bye God". Mr Stumblucci heard so many farts, *sonva bitches, o cazz and bestias,* that he instinctively stayed in place, and continuously crossed himself and began saying the rosary.

The family looked like a Notra Dame and Army football pile up on the one foot line. The musty wine, vinegary bananas, and standard garlicy house smell overpowered the odor of free floating flatulence.

One should not be critical. Just before this family gathering, the family had eaten antipasto with an *insalata* dressed with wine vinegar and oil. The *primo piatto* (first dish) was stew made from *cucucciel* (zucchini), garlic, dandelion greens and potatoes. The main course was *pasta* and *fasuol*. Heavy potent red kidney beans and macaroni.

Babio was at school and did not partake in the family togetherness.

Now you may depressively conclude that this incident was a major tragedy but ———— it was not! The Stumblucci family had over the years, become accustomed to falling and farting. The major *disgrazia* (misfortune) ———— did not become obvious until three months later.

Those "sonva bechee frutta flies" with dispatch, immediately migrated from the dining room upon being exposed to the noise.

In their migrating itinerary, the fruit flies made their first stop in the kitchen. All 300 generations swarmed over the left-over luncheon *insalata* (salad). Those little tiny bestia not only picked up the aceti germs from those rotten bananas but they fooled around with the vinegar in the salad. After this brief stop the "smalla sonva bitchee" smelled the fermenting wine and jetted down to the cellar.

Stumblucci's had followed the ways of the old country to make wine. There were six, 50-gallon white oak, used, whiskey casks in the primary fermenting stage. The bungs were left open to allow the impurities to bubble through the round holes of the barrels. The pretty white purple impurities foamed over the top and ran down the sides of the barrels. Neighborhood belief was that Muscatel wine "wasa so stronga, dat noa germs coulda spoil ita". The "sonva beechee frutta flies" got to the barrels, spread the *aceto* bacteria, and disproved the commonly held belief.

Three months later, one of the greatest tragedies that had ever befallen the neighborhood was learned. The Stumblucci's were hit with the greatest of disgrazia. They had fermented 300 gallons of vinegar.

The incident was so grieved that the neighborhood went into deep mourning. Everyone was in a state of stunned shock and petrified grief. Even the kids didn't dare laugh about such a horrible happening.

Every family empathized with the Stumblucci's. For every family had a barrel, now and then, turn to vinegar. These incidents were never revealed, they were a well kept family secret. A skeleton in the closet. Children were sworn to *le segreto de la casa* (the secrets of the house).

Community compassion came through. Saint Lucy, St. Pergrine and novenas would take care of crooked eyes and feet, but the neighborhood Christiani would help support the Stumblucci paisani for the next year.

Every time Zio Gino did plumbing or other odd jobs, two or three gallons of wine were added to the pay. Families not only came from the East side, but also from the Lovejoy, Fillmore, Delevan and West side Italian sections of town to give work to Zio Stumblucci. Wine always accompanied payment.

Wine was sent over requesting that the Stumblucci's taste and evaluate various homemade wines. These requests were made with coution, so as not to embarrass or shame the family. Peppino the shoemaker, commented *"data familee hasa gotta very sensatevee bocche* (mouths). Goda gave disa to da familia to make upa for da mistake, He made wita derr crooked eyes anda feeta."

The truth, the Stumblucci's had such varied comprehensive wine gifts bestowed, that they became wine-tasting experts. For years afterwards, they were called upon to evaluate neighborhood wines.

Surprisingly, the family never became outwardly angry with me. They always wished me well in my studies and continued to welcome me into their home.

Lest I leave you in a state of deep melancholia as a result of this tragic story, I would like to add a post script.

Alfredo was drafted, at the beginning of the second world war. Within six weeks he was expediently discharged. He couldn't march or shoot straight.

A special delivery letter was sent to the local draft board pleading that no other Stumblucci family member be drafted.

As a result, Alfredo got a job in the defense industry. Soon after, his brothers and sister were also hired at Bell Aircraft Systems.

The family was found to have a precious hidden talent. They all became quality control inspectors. Because of their focal visual acuity, they could evaluate small precision parts. Since this job required being seated, their crooked feet were of no hindrance. Actually, they were so proficient, they saved the company many manhours at the end of the war they received many distinguished awards.

Giovonella was also hired at Bell, but in the drafting graphic arts department. With crooked eyes and artistic talents, she was able to draw precision parts for the tool and die making section of the company.

Babio remained in school. He, like his brothers, became a city wide 100 yard dash track star. Years later, the coaching world recognized that being pigeon-toed contributed to a runners intense combustible start power.

Babio received both scholastic and athletic scholarships. Eventually, he became a dentist and specialized in making false teeth. His disgrazia, artistic talents and intelligence, combined to make him renowned throughout the eastern seaboard. He received special commissions from dignitaries to make authentic appearing false teeth.

Fortunately, my cure failed. Had I succeeded, the Stumblucci's would have ended up without distinctions and awards. Peppino said: "Santa Lucia answered allova thosea novenas ina mixed upa way",

Zio and Zia Stumblucci grew old together. Zia Madelaine cooked all week in preparation for her family's routine Sunday visit. The dining room was always filled. The grandchildren, noisy, fun-loving, exuberant, had the run of the house. Saint Lucy and votive lamps were still in their place. But the candle was never lit. Their four daughters-in-law and son-in-law had straight eyes and feet. Their grandchildren were not very good copiers. The Disgrazia did not befall the grandchildren.

Zio Stumblucci worked in his vegetable garden in the summer. His reading and writing ability became known to the neighborhood. During the winter months, in particular, he wrote letters to the old country for his neighbors.

A black family now occupied the house next door. Howard, a petite, gregarious, likeable four year old black boy lived with his working mother and grandmother. His father was dead. Howard liked to work with Zio Stumblucci in his garden. With his broken English and slow, quiet voice, Zio taught Howard about vegetables, flowers and grapevines. He always cautioned Howard not to step on the tomatoes and peppers, and to clean his muddy feet before going into the house.

In the summer evenings, Zio and Zia sat on the front porch licking ice cream and saluted their neighbors who respectfully returned the salutations.

Howard stood between Zio's legs, or sat on his lap licking ice cream. When Howard became tired, he, without hesitation, crawled into Zio

Stumblucci's ever receptive lap. He was embraced, rocked and peacefully

fell asleep.

Your Amico

Angelo

Chapter 5

Instigatore Sarto

Five A.M. on Saturdays during the Summer months, they met in front of Sarto's Tailor Shop, preparing to go woodchuck hunting. BeBe Carnivale

drove his 1932 two door Studebaker. They sat in their usual spots. Sarto sat in front next to BeBe. Campione sat to the right, in the back. Angelo sat

between his father's legs, in the middle. On the left were three full bushels of food and wine. By the time dawn's warm sunlight came over the horizon, they were traveling past a rustic stone hedge in East Aurora, heading for the spring-fed Camping Area in Bliss, New York. When they came to the top of hills, BeBe cut off the engine and coasted down to save gas. Monoforte, always observing could distinguish rocks and logs from woodchucks. This prevented us from indiscriminately stopping to shoot stumps.

They set up camp and pulled out the bushels of food. The hunters went out in search of game. Sarto hunting for half a day, usually came back with two or three chucks. BeBe did the same. Manofort usually retrieved eight or ten after hunting for most of the day. Campione seldom, if ever, shot his sixteen gauge external hammered, artistically designed, dustless shot gun. He was brought along to *contare e raccontare la storia, per allegrezza* (to sing and tell fun stories). Additionally, he eviscerated, pelted, and removed glands from the woodchuck's fore legs. Without gland removal, the animal could not be cooked or eaten. The resulting odors resembled a skunk in defensive posture. By the way, the reader has discerned by now, Campione never once shot a woodchuck.

About midday, they all gathered for lunch which lasted for hours. A bushel basket filled with fried coffee-colored pork and beef meatballs stuffed with bread crumbs, mint, garlic *vasncola* and *ptrsin* (basil and parsley) and pounds of boiled ham, sicilian olives, prosciutto, chunks of *caciocavallo* and *stozzi* of baked homemade bread was in reach. All of this was enriched with a blend of foxy New York Concord and California

Zinfandel wine. Fresh fruits and nuts ended lunch, followed by slumber and card playing during the heat of the day.

Before sundown while on their way home, something happened At the intersection of Elk and Seneca Streets one hot sizzling macadam day, their tires went flat. Twenty-nine patches melted off the tire tubes. Sarto's sons, Samuel and Frank came to the rescue in their rumble seat Hupmobile car and replaced all of the patches. Campione entertained us with his singing and story telling, enriched by a background chorus of laughter.

Monoforte hunted rabbits in the fall of the year. His two, beagle hunting dogs were named Jack and Julia. These dogs were so good at tracking and retrieving rabbits, that they were borrowed by many neighborhood hunters. They never were loaned to *Medegon* hunters because Jack and Julia only understood Italian. Many dogs in the neighborhood only understood Italian. If dogs didn't *capish* (understand) Italian, it was obvious that they were *Medegon* dogs.

On Thursday evenings, the hunters, *paisani* and *amici* joined together at Sarto's eight foot linoleum covered oval table. The woodchucks had soaked for almost a week. Replenished by dripping water from the bathtub faucet *ent na tina gross* (a big pot). The carcasses evolved into a vibrant pinkish cream color. Always present in the bathtub were also assorted pots of water soaking dried *lpini, fava, ceci, fasuli,* and *baccala.* Angelo wondered then and still wonders if people ever used the bathtub.

Thursday morning, Peppina, Sarto's sister-in-law, simmered the woodchucks in a sauce of homemade tomatoes and tomato paste, garlic, olive oil, vasenicolla, peppers and onions over a low gas flame on a black cast iron stove. Next to the stove, a commercial mixer prepared dough for eighteen loaves to be baked in a full sized pizza oven. This number of loaves was made three times per week to serve the ten children of the Sarto family, and paisani and friends who were frequent visiters.

After sharing woodchuck alla caciatore, they regularly enjoyed Concetta's cheese cake for dessert, made by Sarto's daughter. The cake was made with one bottle of red cherries, a large can of pineapple, a large can of peaches five pounds of ricotta, three cups of sugar, eight eggs and three cups of flour. Ingredients were placed in a pie crust in a 325° oven for about one hour. Dessert included 1 ½ ounces of espresso made with an Italian, black, ground bean in a Neopolitan *macchinetta* flip drip pot.

It is very doubtful if the reader will ever be able to indulge in the beatifically blissful rapture of woodchuck and will probably have to settle for third best chicken alla *cacciatore*. The table was cleared; the hunters and *amici* played *briscola*. Sarto and BeBe were partners playing against Monoforte and his son Angelo.

Players split the deck, the highest card drawn became the dealer. Counterclockwise the dealer dealt each player three cards. The thirteenth card was trump and placed face up next to the undealt deck in the center of the table. Winning three out of five *rages*, meant winning the game. To win a *rage*, the winning team needed 61 points. Point cards are Ace - 11 points, Three - 10 points, King - 4 points, Queen - 3 points, Jack - 2 points. A fascinating part of the game was discreetly sending a partner facial or body signals when a trump card was in hand. A danger to be avoided was an opponent observing a signal. Partners sometimes made up their own signals. A common system is:

Ace -stretch the lips over teeth

Three -distort the mouth to one side

King -glance upwards

Queen -show the tip of the tongue

Jack - shrug one shoulder

The winner of the *Briscola* game became the *boss*. He could elect whoever he wished to be *Sotto boss*,(under boss). Boss sometimes gave *sotto boss* the privilege of deciding who could drink wine. If the *boss* agreed, he accepted his *sotto boss's* decision. If the boss did not, he cancelled the privilege and decided himself. This meant the boss could drink all the wine, share it with *sotto boss* onlookers and even the losing players. If the *boss* and *sotto boss* elected to drink all the wine themselves, the losers vengefully planned to win the next game and return the insult. The winners mouthed many proverbs. With the first glass of wine "*Un giorno senza vino come un giorno senza sole*" (a day without wine is like a day without sun). With the second glass of wine "*acqua fa male. il vino fa canta*", (water is harmful; wine makes one sing) and finally to further tease the losers "*La bivori non misurata; fa l'uomo asino*", (drunkenness makes an ass of man). The winners were saying, be happy that you lost the game and wine.

Sarto lived next door to the Allhands Saloon and strip club. Sarto's son built a clam stand contingent with a parking lot that belonged to Allhands Saloon. Bushels of discarded clam shells were retrieved once a week by garbage collectors. Did these used clams attract flies? Yes! Yes!

Sarto had fly swatters in every room. Fly catchers were hung from the ceiling in the kitchen, dinning and living rooms. Sticky paper was encased in a 3/4 diameter, 2 inch long spool. The paper was pulled out, unfurld 18 inches or longer. Hundreds of flies caught their feet on the sticky paper. Every house had fly swatters and fly catchers.

On the other side of Sarto's brick building, lived Manoforte. Adjacent to Manoforte's brick two family home lived Gino Stumblucci in a wood- frame, two family house. Angelo spent a great deal of time with Sarto and his family of ten children.

On a hunting trip, Campione was cleaning woodchucks, adjacent to a main highway, which paralleled a railroad track. Sarto and Angelo were sitting on a blanket a short distance away. In the background was a clump of trees. Sarto told Angelo *"Va Spara Campione, Un cul"*. Angelo went behind a tree, and while Campione was bending over, he shot him in the ass with a Daisy air rifle "bebe" gun. Campione, stood up and screamed *"Mi sono sparato! Mi sono sparato!"* ("Someone shot me. Someone shot me"). Campione pulled down his pants and separated his slit long white underwear.

Sarto said in the Calabreze dialect *"Nont met paura"* (Don't be afraid). "I willa remova da bullet." With a long bread knife in hand, he told Campione to stay bent over while he removed the bullet. Of course there was no bullet nor was the bebe from the air pressured gun sufficiently powerful to pierce the pants let alone the long white woolen underwear. Sarto, pretending to remove the bullet said *"e finita"* (it is done).

Campione turned seeing the huge long knife and thanked Sarto, *"grazie"*. By this time Campione realized that it was Angelo who shot him. "Soniema bitcha, bastia, Angelo" biting his two fingers between clenched teeth. *"Aspetta quando PaPa returno dalla caccia"* (wait till your father comes back from hunting). *"Hea willa giva a youa calc in cul"* (kick in the ass). For *"la mea ferita al culo"* (my wounded ass).

Sarto intervened and explained that Angelo was just a young boy and didn't know what he was doing. "Donta tella Manoforte, Angelo *e molto adolorato*", (he is very sorry) Campione grumbled but never told Monoforte. Sarto put on sad facial expression and winked at Angelo. Campione refused to talk to Angelo for hours. On their drive home, Campione talked about his son Gaetano, who recently arrived from Italy. Angelo said he knew Gaetano well, for he translated Italian into

English for his son at PS #6. Campione smiled and carried on an Italian

conversation with Angelo. Sarto was asked by the passengers in the car

when he and his wife Rosina came to America? Sarto explained that at the

age of 17, He emigrated from Monteleone, Calabria, arriving in the U.S. in

June of 1903. He departed from Naples on the ship *"Citta D. Milano"*. At

the age of 14, Rosina his wife came to the to the U.S. from Caterina, Sicilia.

Rosina was accompanied by her older sister Peppina, on the ship *"Alceria"*

from Naples, Italy.

A year after Rosina arrived in 1907,  she met and

married Sarto in Buffalo, NY. Rosina was 15, Sarto was

21. Peppina, never married, living her entire life with her

sister, brother-in-law, and eight nephews and two nieces.

Sarto and Rosina were adept at reading and writing in English

and Italian, which was very unusual in the neighborhood. Sarto read "Il

Progresso" every day. He was up to date with every happening in Italy and

shared this news with Amici at Peppino's.

Sartorial skills were learned in Italy as an apprentice to a master

tailor in his hometown of Monteleone, Calabria. Townspeople realized that

Sarto superceded his master teacher and brought him all the work he wanted.

This was before Sarto migrated to *bella* La merica.

After a few years in Buffalo, Sarto opened his own tailor shop in

a three story brick building in between Allhands saloon and Monoforte's

house. The taylor shop had sufficient space for measuring suits and coats

and had a steam machine for pressing clothes. Light came in to the shop from

front ceiling to floor window panes. Daughter Concetta

did many of the repairs on older suits, including making

artificial cuffs on worn out pants bottoms. Sarto never handled kidnaped

dry cleaning.

Sarto did all his work on the third floor where he had bright lights. An elastic banded green transparent cap, shielded light while he worked. Occasionally, he would open a front window, allowing him to view his friends in Peppino's shop.

Sarto's skills were well known throughout the city. Many of his customers were police officers, lawyers, and city officials. Form fitting blue serge suits for police were distinguishable as *speciale* work of Sarto. His coats, made for lawyers and city fathers, were noticeable for their black velvet covered collars.

When, Felomena Bue's husband Scuscabiell was arrested for moonshining, she immediately consulted with Sarto for a prominent lawyer. The connection was made by Sarto. The Irish lawyer, Mr. Condon, was able to get a reduced sentence for Scuscabiell Bue. He had to serve one year in jail and was released, after eight months for good behavior.

CRISTMAS, FEAST OF THE SEVEN FISHES

Christmas was a magnificent happy occasion for the Sarto and Amici families. Sarto ordered a fifty gallon barrel of seafood from Boston,

Massachusetts. Chipped ice was packed with the fish, crustaceans and shellfish.

It was not unusual for eels to be alive. Eels can live on land for awhile by breathing through their skin. They were put into Sarto's bathtub, swimming around pots filled with *bacala*. *It* took four to seven days to draw out bacala's protective salt. The cod fish swelled to its normal size and was ready to put into sauce. *Bacala* was also fried or baked *mollicato* (with bread crumbs).

The feast of the seven fishes celebrated the birth of Jesus. Bringing family, relatives, *combari,* and *comari* together for a *cena della vigilia,* (Christmas eve supper). *La Cena* continued from early evening until at least 3:00 a.m. Christmas day. Sarto claimed the seven fishes signified the seven sacraments. Other Amici (friends) made different interpretations. Interpretations were of little consequence. Being together with love and affection for each other was the purpose of the celebrating feast of the seven fishes.

Sarto's first course started the dinner, and consisted of an *antipasto of mozzarella, gorgonzola, provolone*, roasted sweet and hot peppers, olives artichoke hearts, homemade crusty bread and white wine.

Fruit of the sea, fish salad is the second course made with lobster, calamari, clams, oysters, mussels, celery and red marinara sauce, that contained white wine.

Fried fish was next. Bloated *bacala* fried and baked with *mollicato* was prepared with *pepperoni all'aceto, noci, uva secca, e pane mollicato* (vinegar and peppers, nuts, raisins and bread crumbs).

Captone followed. Large female eels, which can grow to sixty inches and have a life span of twelve years, are stuffed with bread crumbs, eggs, cheese, seasoned with basil, garlic, pepper and then finally baked.

Angel hair pasta, covered with clams, mussels, oysters in an *aglio e olio* (garlic and oil) sauce was the fifth course.

The sixth course consisted of baked *merluzzo*, white fish with lemon juice.

Finally, before midnight, black sauce over linguine made with *calamar* ink pods. A cup of the fish juice is set aside. Parsley, garlic, celery flakes, oregano and black pepper are fried with a cup of olive oil until browned. Tomatoes are smashed by hand and simmered for a half hour.

One quart of tomatoes equals out to a twelve ounce volume of tomato paste.

Olive oil, which has been browned, is placed in the simmered red paste.

Finally, the black ink pods inside the calamari are melted in a cup of the

fish juice, passed through a strainer and put into the red sauce which now

converts it into "black sauce".

All Attended Midnight Mass, except Peppina, who prepared an after

Mass meat menu.

Father Farella celebrated the St. Lucy's twelve o'clock Christmas

Mass. The church was decorated with a life sized *Presepio*. St Francis of

Assisi originated the Presepio, a reconstruction of the Jesus nativity in the

manger. This custom has carried on through the ages in many Italian homes.

Presepios are set on a table in a corner of the living room, constructed lovingly

and carefully by children of the household with no two being alike.

This once a year, special occasion

Mass, had a choir of children trained and led

by Vito Bue. Accompaniment for the choir

was a violin, viola, chela, which were played by friends of Vito, who French

bowed a double bass. Some members of the High Tones combo group volunteered as backup. Eugeno played the organ, Umberto Squaliacum, a muted trumpet, with Carlo Sarto offering rhythm on a brushed snare drum.

The Melodic Chorus of children sang *E Nato Gesu*, (Jesus is born), *Buon Natale,* (Merry Christmas), *Notte Sacra*, (Silent Night), *La Ninna Nanna A Gesu*, (Lullaby to Jesus), *La Stella Di Betlemme*, (The Star of Bethlehem), *Alla Luce D'una Stella*, (A light of a Star), *Cantico D'Amore*, (Melody of Love) and *Campane Di Natale*, (Christmas Bells).

After midnight Mass, Sarto, his family, friends, relatives, *combare, comari* walked to his house to eat homemade sausage, fried peppers, and bread, while drinking red wine. Preparations Peppina had made.

They played *sette mez* (7 ½) a card game, for pennies which was really a circumstance that allowed continued joking, stories, laughter and singing of Christmas songs. By 3 or 4 a.m. guests walked home.

Gifts for children were not given on Christmas day, rather children waited for January sixth. The day the three kings followed the star to bring gifts to baby Jesus. La Befana, the good witch, rode her broomstick, crawled down chimneys to present gifts to children.

During the Christmas season alcoholic Gallo was invited and welcomed by the Sarto family even though he was a constant irritant to his neighbors. As a result, he was often provoked by people. The following story is an example of Gallo being harassed.

Gallo's Hat

One summer day, when Sarto wasn't busy working, he sat on his front stoop, joined by Angelo. Italian stories, jokes by Sarto were appreciated by Angelo. *"Guarda"* (look) pulling his right lower eyelid with his right index finger, Peo La Leggeria, who lived down the street, is approaching. A supposedly single man from Quadri, Aquilla, Abruzzi. There were rumors that he abandoned his "white widow" wife in his *citta* (town). Pio, who worked as a street cleaner for the city, starting work at 5:00 a.m. ending his day by late morning. Pio had yellow orange hair, that he dyed with hydrogen peroxide He looked peculiar. An Italian man from the *Mezzogiorno* with yellow orange hair. Pio's nicknames were plentiful. "Fish" because he caught a fish with his bare hands. He named the duce trump card in *briscola* the water boy, which led to another nickname "Water Boy". Usually he was known as Gallo *Chicchiricki*, rooster in English. The nickname that riled him was *"Biondino"* (Blondie).

Strutting with a wide work shovel on his shoulder, he was a *spaccone* (show off) with his brand new straw hat. Sarto as usual, the instigator, advised Angelo to call him *Biondino* making sure Angelo was across Swan Street in front of Peppino's shoe shop. *"Biondino! Biondino!"* Angelo shouted. Pio was enraged. He couldn't run across the street after Angelo, so he took out his anger on his brand new straw hat. Pio threw his hat on the sidewalk, smashing it with his shovel, cursing in Italian and English. *Sona ova bitcha, bestia,,* hitting his right open hand against his left biceps making his left forearm and hand rise up. Sarto, appeased Pio an alcoholic by inviting him for a large glass of concord *la brusca,* foxy homemade wine.

SECOND WORLD WAR

At Peppino's shop, the amici (friends) discussed the war in Europe. They questioned if the United States would enter into combat with Hitler. The question was answered on Sunday December 7, 1941 when Pearl Harbor was infamously bombed by the Japanese. President Franklin Delano Roosevelt declared war the following day. Even though questions of loyalty were raised by Medegons, history revealed that Italian Americans were the largest group that served in the armed forces.

Sarto hung five blue stars in his front window depicting that five of

his boys were in the service. One son received the purple heart for being

wounded. Luckily Sarto did not hang any golden stars, which portrayed

death of loved ones. The neighborhood hung many gold stars. Within a few

blocks from Sarto's, on South Division near Michigan, Morango's son died

in Sicily. On Swan Street near Pine, Barenaccio's

son, died in Sicily. Joseph Gentile's son, Pasquale,

who lived on South Division near Cedar died at

Mount Casino, barely fifty kilometers from his birth place, Frosolone.

Out of this devastation, the GI Bill allowed Sarto's sons and many

other neighborhood veterans to attend college.

Ralph Sam

Dominic

Billy

Charles

Chapter 6

Falcone

SICILIA

Un'occhio

One Eyed Bookie and the Woodchuck

A short, mustached, thin man with untidy clothes walked up Swan Street and always stopped at Peppino's shoe shop. He wore a wrinkled white shirt, buttoned to the top, a dark blue, pinstriped suit jacket, a pair of brown corduroy pants and smoked half a De Nobeli cigar. Now this may not seem unusual, but it must be noted that what made his sartorial appearance distinguishable was a black patch over his right eye. You guessed it! He had one eye, which led to his *sopra nome* (nickname) being Un'occhio. In fact, neighbors only knew him by Un'occhio and not by his legal Christian name.

His one eye didn't hinder his profession as a bookie for the Italian numbers.

Upper east side neighbors were acquainted with the one- eyed bookie, betting pennies daily to win the Italian numbers lottery.

Un'occhio walked into Peppino's to pick up bets. Interpreting dreams into numbers was considered the most promising method to bet numbers.

Peppino had a limited library in his shop. An Italian English dictionary, an anti-Mussolini volume, and above all and most important Deni's Italian dreams to numbers conversion book. Didn't Mrs Palangelo, who lived upstairs from Liotta's chicken store win $500.00 when she dreamt of her grandmother and played her house number:405. Mrs. Palangelo, dreamt of her grandmother a second time a week later and played 405 again and won $600.00. This is definite proof that dream conversion is the way to play and win the numbers lottery. The entire neighborhood knew the scientific logic of this system. Every household had a Deni's dream conversion book bought at Norbito's tobacco and newspaper store at Swan and Pine streets for one dollar and sixty cents. Medegon's played the numbers requesting that Italian neighbors translate their American dreams into numbers from Deni's Italian book. Signor Deni became a multimillionaire from the commissions he earned with his one and only book. This allowed Deni to travel and gamble at the Italian, French and Monaco Rivieras.

Un'occhio picked up bets every day and occasionally returned to pay winners. He prayed every day and at Sunday Mass to St. Jude patron saint of lost causes that there would be winners. Un'occhio received 10% of the winnings.

On a sunny day Un'occhio's appearance became even more peculiar. Attached to a rope, which he held in his left hand was a live woodchuck. Neighbors laughed aloud as Un'occhio strolled to collect bets. Agreeing neighbors said *"e pazzo, e pazzo, e pazzo"* (he is crazy, crazy, crazy).

He walked into Peppino's. Manoforte, Sarto, Sqagliacum, Stumbolucci, and Filomena Bue, happened to be in the shop. Laughter was loud and spontaneous. Some Amici slapped their thighs. Others put their hands together as in prayer, moving hands up and down transmitting *"che cosa fa"* (what the hell are your doing)?

Un'occhio was not embarrassed or slighted. He was there to pick up bets. Manoforte and Sarto were long time woodchuck hunters. Monoforte emphasized "youa cannota traina a woodchucka, becusa its parta of da rat famiglia. Youa seea da teeta ona da sides of da mouta, daya needa too bea sharpeneda alla da time". Sarto reinforced Manoforte's warning. Un'occhio

95

paid no heed to the advise. He continued his rounds in the neighborhood, woodchuck roped to Un'occhio.

The woodchuck was kept in a makeshift wooden box in his bedroom, kitchen, bathroom flat on the second floor of a building owned by the "Greek". On the third floor, the dentist, Dr. Meranti had offices. Street level there was an Italian Greek import food store. Sawdust covered the

floor making it easier for broom clean up. Four barrels were filled with a variety of olives. Black shriveled Sicilian, dark purple amfissa, ioonian bright green and balsamita almond shaped dark purple. In one corner was a barrel of olive oil that customers could spigot draw from, provided thay used their own bottles. One section was a meat market with carcasses hung in a walk- in cooler. Dry fish *baccala* and *pesce stocco* were boxed in open topped wooden crates. A basket, held *babaluci* (snails). A palm interlaced cover, pressed hard on the basket prevented snails from crawling out. Most magnificent was the embossed galvanized tin ceiling from which hung *provolone, salami, capocolla, caciocavallo, proscuitto* which contributed to the beatific aroma of an enormous anti pasto. Two sons of Sarto, Ettore and Luigi worked for the Greek as clerks.

One day, Un'occhio, walked into Peppino's without his roped woodchuck, Wella. "Che succiess" what happened? *"Addo sta la woodchucka"*, (where is the woodchuck)? Accompanied by up and down movements of pointed up clumped fingers. *"Curitu, curritu"*, in Sicilian. (Wella ran away). Smirking laughter ensued. Monoforte said *"mo comenza ru problema"* (Problems will start soon) The prediction of Monoforte was accurate.

Niagara Falls raided the Greek import store. Out of nowhere water dripped through the galvanized tin embossed ceiling. During the night hours while the store was closed, water dripped all over the *provolone, salami, capocolla, prosciutto, caciocavallo* in fact, all over the ceiling hung

97

food. Sawdust reeked with soaking water. *Bacala, pesce stucco* bloated and floated. Guess what! Snails managed to get out of the wet slippery palm basket top. *Babaluci* were crawling clinging on the walls, ceiling, and hanging anti pasta food stuffs. Mr. Stenopolis, the owner panicked when he opened the front door. Soaking sawdust raced by him, over the threshold. Water kept floating out. Ettore and Luigi ran to Gino Stumbolucci's house as directed by their Greek boss. Gino was tending his tomato garden. Imploring zio Gino *"fa subito"* (hurry). Niagara Falls was happening at the Greeks. Gino grabbed a long metal rod from his shed. The shaft had a welded lug at the lower end and a crossbar welded to the top so it could be turned. With heavy breathing, Gino, Ettore and Luigi ran a block to the import store. Gino lifted a cast iron cap of the water control valve system embedded in the sidewalk adjacent to the store wall. He pushed the long poled wrench down the four inch wide pipe and fitted the bolt perfectly with the lug end. He twisted the top "T" bar clockwise, turning the water off in the entire building.

Kids from all over the neighborhood peered through the large pane glassed windows. It really looked like Niagara Falls! Amusingly they stayed until the water was shut off making them late for school.

After a few hours, Niagara Falls stopped dripping from the second story apartment into Stenopolis' store. With the water shut off, the store remained closed.

The catastrophic truth was finally discovered. *Wella*, the "god dammed" woodchuck, sharpened her incisor teeth by making holes in the lead water pipes. This brought on Niagara Falls with its full disastrous splendor.

Un'occhio explained at Peppino *"Bedda Madre"* (holy mother of God), "data sonva bitcha bruttu bastardie *Wella*, costa mea mora den $1000.00". Gino Stumblucci was paid to repair and replace all of the lead pipes with galvanized pipes. It took days of work. Plus, Un'occhio had to pay for sawdust, *babaluci, provolones, salami, capocolla, caciocavallo, proscuitto*, olives, bloated *bacala, peshe stucco* and all the food stuffs spoiled with water. The only things saved were can goods, meat in the walk-in cooler, barreled olive oil and grating cheese that was glass covered. All of these went on sale at cost. Clerks had to find all of the *babaluci* and hang the new food products from the ceiling and spread clean sawdust after washing the walls and floor.

Dr. Meranti, the dentist on the third floor cancelled patients and went on vacation to the Canadian side of Niagara Falls, until repairs were completed. The dentist wanted to charge Un'occhio for the dental patients he lost but settled for a year's worth of free nickle bets a day of Italian bookie numbers.

The question asked by Manoforte, raising his palms and shrugging his shoulders, *Do sta Wella cu li dente* (where is Wella with the sharp teeth)?"

Days passed, everything was going *"bene"*(well). Un'occhio collecting numbers, and being teased by neighbor *"com sta Wella"* (how's Wella)? Embarrassed, he gave no response. The ribbing was felt.

One early morning, about 4:00 a.m. Un'occhio got out of bed to take a leak. As he walked into the unlighted bathroom, he could barely see Wella near the toilet bowl. Half awake, he quietly tiptoed back to his closet retrieving his 20 gauge shotgun. Returning, he sighted and aimed at Wella with his one good eye. Bam! Bam! He fired both barrels of the shot gun, squarely blowing apart the toilet and feeding water pipe. You guessed it! Niagara Falls gloriously flowed again.

Un'occhio was about to run to Gino Stumblucci's house in his long white ass split *mutande (*underwear). Fortunately or unfortunately, Gino pulled his pants over his underwear, put on his shoes. a hat, and ran as fast as he could. Arriving at Stumblucci's house, he banged on the door. He could have walked in, for no one locked their doors in the neighborhood. It was totally safe. No robberies had been or were expected to be committed. Out of respect, he remained outside the door and continued banging. Stumblucci heard the noise at the door. Gino assumed a *"briacone"* (drunk) from the Allhands Saloon, a few doors away was knocking at his door at this early a.m. hour. He ignored the knocking. Un'occhio kept banging! banging! Hollering *"Aiutami! Aiutami! Aiutami!"* (Help me! Help me! Help me!) Stumblucci half asleep, dressed in his red long ass split *"mutanda"*opened the door. Un'occhio anxiously, nervously, stuttering, stammering explained that Niagara Falls flowed a second time. It was necessary that Gino come and shut the water off at the Greek's store.

Gino, put on his pants, shoes hat and went to the shed in back of his house retrieving the crossbar lug ended rod tool. Together they ran down Swan Street in the predawn hour of 5:00 A.M. Stumblucci lifted the cast iron cap of the water control system, pushing the long poled wrench down the four inch wide pipe, fitting the bolt perfectly with the lug end. Twisted the "T" bar clockwise turning off the water to the entire building.

After a few hours Niagara Falls stopped dripping from the second story apartment into the Greek's store. At 7:30 a.m. Stenopolis with his clerks behind him opened the door. Surprise! Surprise! Sawdust floating on water flowed out the threshold doorway. Impossible! No one could believe this. Again, a second time, Niagara Falls controlled the store. It could not be, but it is. Stumblucci replaced the lead pipes with galvanized steel pipes. What really happened? Eventually the true story was revealed. An embarrassed Un'occhio with red cheeks and down cast eyes explained that his shotgun blew up the toilet and feed in water pipe. Certainty that he hit his "sonabitcha bestia Wella", was unknown?

Water dripped through the embossed galvanized tin ceiling. All of the *prosciutto, salami, capocolla, caciocavallo, provolone* were dripping wet, including the counter top, 40 pound wheel of *parmigiano* grating cheese. *Pesce stucco baccala* again bloated and floated. Olives flowed out the water filled barrels onto the swampy waterlogged sawdust floor. *Babaluci* were happily crawling over walls, ceilings and hanging food stuffs. Refrigerated hanging meat carcasses, can goods, ricotta and other cheeses in glass covered display cases were salvageable, at discount prices.

Dr. Meranti was reimbursed ten cents a day for one year to play the Italian numbers. Dr. Meranti closed down his no water practice. This second time, the dentist and his family went to the American side of Niagara Falls, until water was turned on in his third floor dental offices.

Though, Dr. Meranti, was a dentist many neighborhood people went to him if they had medical problems. He was cheaper then going to the medical doctor. His treatment was consistent "Take a laxative every Saturday to clean out body systems thus medical problems would truly be avoided". Every Saturday many neighborhood people took vile tasting castor-oil followed by eating an orange for taste relief. New, better tasting physics were bought including "One, Two, Three Go", in a capped- lemon tasting liquid that fizzled when opened. This laxative was easily found in all stores. Product label information, illustrated a boy running with his left hand holding up knickers, revealing his partially clad behind. The uplifted right hand grasping a roll of toilet paper. The boy was obviously running to the toilet. Even illiterates could find this laxative. In small print was listed the ingredient: magnesium citrate. Some fortunate kids had a laxative, strawberry, vanilla, chocolate soda at Hirch's Drugstore. While

sipping through a straw, they read comic books. Once a month, for a dime,

Famous Funnies could be bought and then traded with friends for other

comic books. Eventually, a superior tasting laxative was discovered——-

chocolate "Exlax". Now it became easily decernable, as to who were the

patients of Dr. Meranti? Saturdays, they were the people who farted the

most.

Manoforte questioned *"Quant la sci pagat, Un'occhio"?*
Communicating the question with up and down movements of pointed up

clumped fingers. (How much did it cost you this time)? Un'occhio, red

faced, replied *"Quattro centu dollaru di menu de la prima vota"* (four

hundred dollars less then the first time). Meaning that Gino Stumblucci

didn't have to replace all of the in wall galvanized pipes, only the pipe

feeding the toilet and a new toilet costing $30.00, at Seneca Plumbing. In

addition, Gino gave him a discount for his frequent jobs, plus the notoriety

the self learned plumber received in the Buffalo Times morning paper and

Buffalo Evening News. Italian newspaper Il Proggresso and Il Curriere

wrote extensive articles about Un'occhio's Niagara Falls, including the

splendid plumbing work of Gino.

What happened to Wella? There were no further Niagara Falls. Wella was never found! Un'occhio and Dr. Meranti's apartments had a terrible smell for months. This odor seemed to originate from the bathroom walls.

Bull Runs Amuck

Swan and Chicago Streets became infamous as result of the Greek Import Store suffering two Niagra Falls tragedies. Infamy continued. "**The Bull that Ran Amuck in Street, Seven Hurt**" was a headline of the <u>Buffalo Times Newspaper</u> on September 1, 1932. The caption read:

"Street Crowds Terrorized by Wild Animal"

Two women, four men and a child are victims of rampage.

The article continued:

Two women, four men and a five year old boy were injured when a wild bull broke loose from a truck this afternoon and terrorized the down town area. Those injured were:

Mrs. Carmella Fracki, of 316 Swan Street. Emergency Hospital with injuries to her back.

Mrs. Josephine Argusano 53 of 292 Swan Street. Cuts and bruises and a wrenched knee.

James Imbo 39 of 307 Swan Street cut and bruised and injuries to his left leg.

Albert Longo, 4922 Kenmore Avenue, in Emergency Hospital, suffering from cuts and bruises, gash in forehead and injuries to right leg.

Rocco Sperduti, 5 of 309 Swan Street, cuts, bruises and internal injuries.

Detective Ford J. Roggero of the Auto Squad cuts and bruises.

Bernard Moni 26 of 420 South Division Street Cuts, bruises and injuries to the abdomen.

Charging through the streets and alleyways of the East Side, the animal left a trail of shrieking and hysterical women and children in its wake. It also left innumerable wrecked fenders where it had crashed into automobiles.

A general call for police radio cars to join the chase was sent out when police were made aware of the animal rush.

Under the direction of Deputy Commissioner Conolly, squads of automobiles carrying detectives and radio men rushed to the vicinity of Swan Street where the Bull was reported seen.

Detectives trailed the bull unable to stop its charge and afraid to shoot for fear of striking pedestrians.

The bull made its fatal mistake when it paused in front of the vegetable section of Stenopolis Import Store.

According to observers, the bull was attracted by a large pile of cabbage in the window and crashed through. It jumped back out and ran into Capozzi's gas station driveway. Detective Guy C. Dewey recognized as one of the ace shots of the Buffalo Police Force, advanced and shot the bull twice through the head. The butcher from Stenopolis Italian Greek Import store, Ettore (Sarto's son) dashed out unsheathed a knife and cut the bulls throat.

This *disgrazia* (catastrophe) was discussed for weeks at Peppino's. Eventually, but slowly, the true facts came out. The Buffalo Times Newspaper article was partially misquoted. What really happened? Buck Jones, this nick name was derived because he owned and stabled horses, including the rag man's horse on Myrtle Avenue. Buck was driving the bull carrying truck owned by Klenck Brothers of Howard Street. Buck Jones stopped the truck in front of Sperduti's grocery store and crossed the street to have a beer at Manzello's Saloon. The bull didn't enjoy the truck not moving, and smashed out the back wooden gate. Rocco, the four- year- old was pulled into the store by his mother. Rocco walked out the side door back onto Swan Street. The bull, having no regard for the boy's littleness, pushed him onto the sidewalk. Friends of the family hollered and screamed, frightening the bull, which ran towards Stenopolis' Italian Greek Import Store. Ettore, Sarto's son, Rocco's mother and Mr. Cappozzi gave their views of what really happened with the runaway bull. Buck Jones in his embarrassment never relayed his story at Peppino's.

Years later Rocco never forgot how he was hit by the bull. He wanted to go up town to the main Erie County library to search out newspaper articles. This was not possible because he didn't have the dates.

About fifty years later, Vincent "Whitey" Albaneza was knocking a wall down in his home. Lo and behold, he found an oxygenated, Buffalo Times Newspaper between the walls. Yes it was the bull story dated

September 1, 1932. He reached Rocco, let him read the orange colored newspaper, but would not give it to the boy hit by the bull.

Rocco told this story to Angelo as they were drinking coffee at the Aromi Coffee Café. Angelo had Lofreddo's Photographic Studio print of a 8X10 inch portrait of Vincent in a blue navy suit holding a prayer book and rosary. This was taken on Vincent's first communion day. Rocco spoke to Whitey Albaneza. (Vincent's nickname Whitey referred to his having blond hair). Whitey agreed and made the trade. The newspaper for the photograph. Rocco's son-in-law, framed the newspaper article and displayed it at Rocco and Mary Sperduti's 50th anniversary.

Un'occhio's eccentric dress, black eye patch and walking *Wella,* the woodchuck, may have had merits. Irish cops from Precinct 2, South Division near Spring Street never stopped, arrested or even acknowledged that Un'occhio was an Italian number bookie. Panzaniello and his two sons, had to pay off the cops so that their bookie enterprise would not be disturbed.

Did Un'occhio make any money considering his two Niagara Falls losses? Well—— judge for yourselves. Eventually, he retired from his profession, buying one of the first brick ranch houses on Potters Road, adjoining Cazenovia Park in south Buffalo. Un'occhio sent for his sister and her family in Falcone, Sicily, his birthplace. Catarina his sister, was born after Un'occhio migrated to the U.S. Catarina and Nando, her husband, arrived in Buffalo with their ten year old son and two teenage daughters. Un'occhio's nieces completed high school at Mount Mercy Academy, eventually becoming registered nurses, working at Mercy Hospital. Geramio, his nephew, completed Timon High School and attended the University of Buffalo School of Engineering. Geramio earned a PHD in civil engineering. Nando, Un'occios brother-in-law, worked as a janitor at Mercy Hospital. They all walked to school and work, needing no money for transportation, except for Geramio who attended the University. Uncle Un'occhio bought a used car for his nephew and paid for all the tuition, fees, and books. Geramio also earned a number of scholarships.

Caterina stayed at home as *casalinga* (housewife) and never learned English. She managed the home for her family and brother who henceforth never had to cook his own meals.

Yearly on September 8th, all the paesani from Falcone, Sicily, came from all over the Eastern United States to hold an enormous *festa* in Buffalo. The visitors never rented hotel rooms, rather slept on mattresses placed on floors in the homes of paesani. Actually, they slept little conversing about the good times they had growing up in Falcone.

Falcone is a village of about 1000 people. It is located on the north shore of the Sicilian island about 20 kilometers west of Messina, in a bay of the Mediterranean Sea called the "Gulfo Di Potti". Two streets make up the village. One road, Via Immaculata, led to the top of the mountain to a group of houses called Casino Di Falcone. Un'occhio's family lived there in an all stone stucco house built into the hillside. From the top of Via Immaculata one could see the ancient cliffs of Tindara, where Greek settlers, and before them, Greek pirates threw down their prisoners of war. The Falconese, as well as their sister village of Tindari, are prideful of their ancient Greek past. Above all, the sanctuary of the Black Madonna in Tindare, is also highly honored by the Falconese. People from all over the world who visit the Black Madonna Sanctuary. On September 8th, the Byzantine Black Madonna Celebration brings back memories, food, singing for the migrated Falconese.

As he aged Un'occhio kept his mustache and DeNobili cigars but never wore a black patch over his missing eye. Stumblucci's dentist son,

Dr. Babio, not only designed famous false teeth, but also designed a glass eye for Un'occhio.

Sarto made Italian styled silk suits for Un'occhio. This meant Un'occio never wore his rag tag "fooling the cops clothes" which he wore while he served as a numbers bookie. He traveled to Peppino's almost daily by walking through Cazenovia Park around the man-made canoeing lake, then took the Seneca Street car to Chicago Street. Un'occhio walked past the Greek import store and had Niagara Falls memories. Then he proceeded past St. Lucy's church, crossed Chestnut Street and walked into Peppino's shop. He wore his Sarto' s real silk suits, white starched shirt, imported Italian silk tie and wide brimmed velvet Borzllino hat. Peppino, Manoforte, Stumblucci, Sarto, Signora  Bue knew more about *Wella* the woodchuck, than they knew about how Un'occhio lost his eye.

Chapter 7

Squagliacum

At the age of 17, Felice had migrated to Brazil with his father, from the hamlet  of Acqueviva, town of Frosolone, Campobasso Abruzzi to work on a coffee plantation. Within a year, he became a foreman because of his adeptness with the Portuguese language. After three years, Felice returned to the village of Acqueviva. He was noted for making

lead handles for butcher knives and hand held hatchets. This resulted in his *sopranome* (nickname) Squagliacum, (lead melter). Delorata became his bride. Actually Delorata was his childhood sweetheart and lived a few doors away from Felice.

Umberto, his brother, had migrated to Dansville, Kentucky where he became a national figure for volunteering and rescuing Floyd Collens from deep within the Mammoth Caves.

Squagliacum and Delorata were called to America by Umberto. They remained in Kentucky for a short time then traveled to Buffalo, New York where there were paesani and jobs. Wide shouldered, big bellied, with a thick white mustach, Squagliacum was always happy, laughing, fitting his name sake Felice, felicity. He bought one of a few, large, inexpensive homes on Exchange Street. To start with, it was next to the Pennsylvania Railroad tracks, which were separated from Squagliacum's two-car garage by a three-foot chain link fence. People sleeping at Felice's house had to become accustomed to the rickety rack noise of trains traveling all hours, day and night. Hearing senses became adjusted for the family and boarders of Squagliacum, but visitors never became accustomed to the noise. The house had no inside toilet! People had to use the *baccausa*, (back house) a two holler outside. A Sears and Roebuck catalog was used for viewing and wiping.

Very early one morning Felice heard a banging noise coming from his storage room. Reasoning that a burglar was trying to break in, he armed himself with a 16 gauge shotgun. He waited ———— waited,———— nothing happened. The banging continued. Squagliacum waited no more. Slowly he opened the storage room door. The pneumatic burglar turned out to be a rat trying to pull a strand of macaroni into his hole. In its mouth the rat had a double strand from a 20 pound box of macaroni. Macaroni in 20 pound boxes were cheaper to buy in bulk. Eighteen inch long macaroni boxes were double the thickness of a silver dollar on the top, bottom and sides. The ends were twice as thick. Double macaroni strands were "u" shaped at one end. The rat persisted and with much effort tried to pull the macaroni, unsuccessfully into his hole. Pasta kept banging at the side of the hole. Felice kicked at the entrance hole. The rat dislodged the mounted double strand and disappeared in the hole. Felice put his outside cat, Tommy, in the storage room. Next day he found the rat—– dead.

At Peppino's, he told the story, (laughter ensued). The *fat* (story) of Squagliacum, rat and macaroni spread throughout the Italian enclave, bringing frequent laughter.

Felice had temporary jobs whenever he could find them. His family would not be disgraced by going on welfare. Niagara Mohawk was about to shut off his lights.. Manoforte, his paesano, and more substantial his comba, heard of the dilemma. Immediately Manoforte paid the bill. Lights stayed

115

on. Being a comba, essentially meant being a close relative. Felice and Delorata baptized Angelo, Manoforte's one and only child. The godparents of Umberto, Squagliacum's son, were Manoforte and his wife, Lucia.

Squagliacum's son, Umberto was named after his Kentuckian much loved brother Umberto Senior. Part time, Umberto worked at "Kidnapped Dry Cleaning". He traveled from house to house, asking in Italian, if the household needed dry cleaning. The clothes were given to Mr. Hellman who was able to get the clothes cleaned at discount. Umberto returned the clothes and received pay as piece work. Young, small, and thin in stature, Italian mothers dragged Umberto into their kitchens exclaiming "*modonna* don'ta youa *mangia,* (eat). Wine mixed with water to prevent skinny Umberto from getting drunk was accompanied with dishes of food. Money he earned by "kidnapped dry cleaning" (more about this later) was given to his family.

Felice Squagliacum had a difficult time finding a full time job during the depression. Working odd jobs including picking, cleaning, selling *cicoria* (dandelions) and *cardun* (burdock) house to house allowed him to feed and care for his family.

Peppino explained that dandelions eaten with olive oil and vinegar sprinkled with parmigiano cheese not only is *diliziosa* but nutritionally healthy, containing vitamins A, B, calcium, phosphorous and iron. In Italy dandelion roots were cleaned, baked, ground up and used as a coffee substitute. Dandelion flowers were made into wine. Amici at Peppino's were astonished to learn of the many nutrients of the dandelion weed, which they had eaten since they were children. What they couldn't understand — why did the *medegons (Americans)* hate dandelions? Pretty yellow flowers, a joy to see.

Felice was not able to find work during the depression years. His family assisted by making money during summer working as migrant farm workers.

Delorata, Angelella, Anna, and Umberto went to Masacio's truck farm during June, July, and August as migrant workers, to pick fruit, vegetables and hoe his fields. Umberto skipped "Kidnaped Dry Cleaning" during those summer months.

In the early part of June, Masacio picked up families with his truck, taking them to his farm. Delorata, her three children, Umberto Angelella, and Anna, loaded the truck with two dressers, clothes in bags, cooking/eating utensils, mattress covers, and toilet paper. A fifty pound bag of flour, a case of pork and beans, 3-20 pound boxes of pasta, home canned tomatoes, polenta flour, pepperoni sticks and gallons of wine were also loaded. Delorata sat in front with the driver. Her children sat in the back of the truck. They did not have to take final exams at School # 6, passing on their average. After an hours drive they arrived at the farm in North Collins. The family moved into the same shack they occupied in previous years.

Twenty-two make shift shacks contiguously tied together for twenty-two families were built from boards and had flat slanted roofs that leaked rain. Knot holes, poorly fitting vertical boards were stuffed with clothes preventing peeking into each others shacks. Umberto hung a rope from wall to wall. Blankets were held on the rope with clothes pins and were described as "the walls of Jerico". This blanket separated Umberto 's sleeping space from his mother and sisters. Each shack was provided with one 60 watt bulb. A hole in the floor with dirt dug out was fitted with a tin box and served as a makeshift ice box. Limited perishable items were placed in the box.

Butter, unpasteurized farm milk, cheese, were held for short periods of time. Mattress covers were filled with corn husks and served as mattresses. Everyday, corn husks were leveled out with an inserted sling shot appearing tree cut limb. Outside each shack was a table, and benches for eating and washing. A mirror, basin, and pail for pumped water were used to wash up.

Underneath the table was a galvanized tub, a wash board, and hand wound wringer used to squeeze out water from washed clothes. Washed clothes were hung out to dry. Once a week the wash tub was used by Delorata and her daughters as a bathtub. Water was heated with one of three outside wood burning stoves. The same lean-to covered stoves were used for cooking. Angelella and Anna were not allowed to go to the creek where boys washed naked.

Farmer Masacio built a brick oven for bread baking. Wood was burned to heat the bricks. The ashes were removed and then bread dough put in. Each family attached a symbol to their bread dough. Confusion as to who owned the baked bread made little difference, as many of the families were related, aunts, cousins, comas.

Delorata, and the other elders, all from Italy's Mezzogiorno spoke Italian. Their children spoke Italian and English. English was spoken when they didn't want their parents to understand. *Baccausa*, two three- holler outhouses, were up the hill. One for boys and one for girls. Twice a week families were assigned to clean the three holers, using brooms, brushes, soap and water to scrub the *baccausa*. Families provided their own toilet paper. While picking in patches, people went behind trees and bushes, resorting to leaves for wiping. Drastic misfortune resulted when poison ivy leaves were unknowingly used for wiping. Unbearable itching was relieved with calamine lotion. Bleeding scratches were disinfected with stinging burning isopropyl rubbing alcohol.

Work started at 6:00 a.m., seven days per week. Trucks took the families to patches for picking. Time off was only if there was drenching rain or patches were not ready to pick. Heavy dew prevented pickers from walking into muddy fields. Pickers waited for the sun to dry out the fields.

Delorata and Umberto hoed fields for ten cents per hour. Angelella and Anna who were not 14, were not allowed to hoe. Strawberries picked by tired back- bending paid one cent per quart. Black berries and raspberries were picked standing up, which caused arm and hand torn scratches. These pickings also paid one cent per pint. Beans and peas paid four cents per pound. Peas were the easiest and most enjoyable to pick. Delorata and her children sat on the ground in their bibbed overalls. Pickers pulled 3 or 4 roots and leaves out of the ground and then separated peas from the bush. Peas and beans were put in baskets, taken to the end of the row, put in burlap bags and weighed. Straw boss, Carmella Popella made sure crops were totally picked.

Carmella punched tickets carried by pickers. Punched tickets indicated the number of quarts, pints and pounds of peas and beans picked.

During lunch hour, water was brought in milk cans and was served with a common scooper. Pork and beans, sardines in cans, peanut butter and jelly sandwiches, pepperoni sticks and *polenta* left over from the night before were brought in a lunch basket. Fruit was dessert.

Once a week, Carmella Popella took orders and traveled by truck to North Collins to buy staples and food.

In the field, mothers hollered *cogli, cogli,* (pick, pick). Pickers talked with each other and sang together, "Old McDonald Had a Farm", "You are My Sunshine" "Red River Valley"also Italian songs *"Santa Lucia", "O'Marie", "Vicin U Mare"*.

At 6:00 p.m., pickers were returned to the shacks by truck. *Pizza fritta* (fried dough) and hot cocoa was supper three times per week. Umberto, Angelella, and Anna called this a dessert supper because the *pizza fritta* was covered with powdered sugar. Other meals included *pasta e* fosool, polenta, macaroni with red sauce, salad and wine.

Horseshoes were played in the evenings. Occasionally, teenagers and children took a half hour walk to North Collins to buy ice cream. At darkness, bonfires were built. Potatoes were roasted. Umberto played the trumpet, Tony Zangera played the mouth organ and Dominic Popella played the sax. There was dancing on the earth.

Girls were protected by mothers and brothers. Mothers warned *"stat attient"* (be careful). The concept was understood. Don't disgrace yourself, your family or neighbors. Never! was there an out of wedlock pregnancy or sexual fooling around. Kissing? Maybe!

Delorata and her children were paid at the end of the summer after submitting their punched cards. They made enough money to buy coal from Signor Amigone for the winter months, school clothes and one family furniture item.

Families were driven home by truck. Delorata bought twelve bushels of tomatoes from Masacio to be canned *bagno maria*, and was also made into paste by being covered with curtains and sun-dried. Canned tomatoes in pop bottles, with salt and basil leaves added, were placed in an oblong copper tub. Each layer of bottles was covered with newspapers. The tub was filled with water and heated to boiling. A two burner portable gas stove, connected by a rubber hose to a gas jet was used to boil the water outside or in the cellar.

Families embraced and kissed each other as they departed the farm. *Auguri, saluti,* (best wishes and good health) until we see each other next year.

Eventually Felice found a job.

Cousin Nunzio, a worker at the Chevy plant on East Delavan Avenue was finally able to get Squagliacum a job. Management, realizing Felices' skill as a gardener assigned him to care for the horticulture grounds of the plant. Squagliacum had skill to cut and trim hedges, and grow flowers. Plus he had the ability to graft roses and fruit trees. He learned all of these skills in Brazil and Italy. Endeared by administrators, he worked three days at their private homes and two days at the plant.

One morning, as administrators arrived at work, they were confronted with a lawn covered with water which eventually seeped into the plant. Plant engineers were called. They brought blueprints listing all the underground pipes. They concluded that an underground pipe had burst. Squagliacum was directed where to dig holes to uncover the broken pipe. Felice dug all day. No broken pipe. After studying their blueprints a second day Squagliacum was told "Dig here". No broken pipe. After studying their blueprints a committee of engineers, administrators studying the blue prints finally arrived at the broken pipe place to dig. *"Nata vote"* (again) Squagliacum dug! dug! dug! A third time. No broken pipe! Three days and no broken pipe. He refilled all the holes planting grass seed where needed.

Squagliacum, was tired of the college educated engineers, *"nun san chell che fan"* (not knowing what they were doing). Digging holes was hard work! Squagliacum went to the bosses and asked "giva mea chanca anda I willa finda da brokina pipa". His wish was begrudgingly given. Using simple thinking, without blueprints, which he couldn't read anyways, Felice searched the grounds. Where he found puddles of water, he knew this was the best place to dig. He waited two days before digging. Why? Couldn't he rest from all the hard work he spent digging holes. After all those *"Goddammeda Medegon"* blueprint engineers didn't know what they were doing. Yes! Yes! He dug and found the broken pipe. Stumblucci, his amici from Peppino's was hired to repair the pipe. Of course, Squagliacum helped his friend, Gino.

The management of the Chevy plant were immensely pleased with their gardener, but not endeared to the engineers with their underground blueprints. Squagliacum was rewarded two days off with pay for finding the broken pipe.

Taking the Delavan IRC bus to Grider Street is where Squagliacum transferred to the South Park bus. This was his daily route home. When he arrived at the Grider Delavan intersection, students from Burgard and Seneca Vocational High Schools were standing ready to make transfers. All the women, men, and students rushed to get on the bus. Missing the bus, meant a 20 minute wait for the next bus. Felice Squagliacum spread out his strong arms saying "Ladies firsta". Women got on and the bus was filled. The door slammed shut. Felice stood red faced embarrassed with arms spread out. Students roared with laughter. Next day, standees were waiting. The bus arrived. Squagliacum spread out his strong arms saying "Felice firsta anda everybodia nexta".

After riding the bus and streetcar Felice realized the importance of having a family car. Squagliacum could not drive. He encouraged his son Umberto to buy a car.

Umberto, with the financial help of two house boarders, Niccolo and Big John bought a car. Niccolo was the cousin of Umberto and nephew of Delorata. Big John was a paesano from Squagliacum's town Acqueviva.

The boarders were generous and giving to Umberto. When Umberto was ill they brought him oranges. They often treated him to movies. The purchased open top car was not a convertible. It just didn't have a top. It that was probably sawed off by the previous owner. Thirty four dollars and fifty cents was the cost of this 1927 Chrysler.

Immediately, Felice and his wife sprinkled salt in all four corners of the car. This omen would prevent accidents. A red *corno*, (an amulet shaped like a horn) was hung on the rear view mirror. This protected the passengers from *malocchio* (evil eye).

Umberto and friends painted the car yellow and covered it with painted comic book characters. Including Mickey and Minnie Mouse, Goofy, Popeye, Olive Oil. Actually, this yellow $34.50 sawed off top car was one of the few cars in the neighborhood. Sorry to say, there were other idiosyncracies to the car. It had a windshield, but only hand turning wipers. Without a top why were hand turning wipers needed? Four umbrellas were carried in the event of rain. The passenger next to the driver had to hold up two umbrellas. One for himself and the other to cover the driver. When it rained the driver drove with one hand and turned the wiper with the other.

By the way, holes were drilled into the floor boards allowing rain to drain out. Everyone in the neighborhood recognized the yellow, comic- book charactered topless car. It was considered a luxury, even though there were other mechanical problems. The brakes didn't always work. If by chance the Chrysler went over 50 miles per hour, which could only happen while going down hill, the fabric gaskets sealing the transmission would burn out. Umberto bought heavy fabric from dirty Mary's on Clinton Street. This store had dusty bolts of cloth piled on each other with every color texture and design. Only garlicky smelling Mary could find what Umberto requested. Umberto made gaskets with six holes for the bolt fittings of the transmission. A half dozen gaskets with bolt wrenches were always carried as a precaution.

Ordinarily, when it rained, the car was parked in his father's garage next to a brand new Packard sedan owned by Peggerio, the pharmacist.

On Wednesdays, Umberto picked up three nuns at St. Lucy's School, driving them to St. Mary's Redemtorist Church on Pine and Broadway to attend Our Lady of Perpetual Help Novena. As he drove one Wednesday, Umberto noticed a wheel roll by his car. Unusual and perplexing with a wrinkled brow, he wondered where the wheel came from. He saw yellow rims. *Madonna* (mother of God) his

back wheel rolled passed him. Unknown to Umberto, his friends repaired

a flat tire and forgot to put the lugs on. Without tipping, leaning or falling

the yellow car rolled forward. Nuns were seated in positions that balanced

and prevented the car from dropping. Umberto continued driving slowly,

attempting to catch up with his rear left tire.

At a stop light, he veered to the right, slid along the curb and stopped

the Chrysler. This was done because the brakes didn't always work. Pleaded

with the nuns, to remain still. He leapt over the driver's side door, ran after

the wheel, rolled it back and replaced it. Umberto tightened it with two lugs,

removed from other wheels. It was a miracle! Our Lady of Perpetual Help

performed the miracle in reparation for the many years the St. Lucy Nuns

made the Novena.

Peppino's amichi talked about the *miracolo* (miracle) of the run away

wheel, analyzing what numbers to play with Un'occhio. Four wheels, two

lugs, three nuns. Four two three and various derivations were played but to

no avail. Nobody won the Italian numbers. The amici however considered

making Mother of Perpetual Help Novenas for numbers miracles. Correct

numbers choices would make them rich winners. After a few days of discussion, they decided not to make the novena. After all they couldn't

miss work to celebrate afternoon novenas.

Squagliacum ran to Panzaniello's house at 2:30A.M., awakening

him, requesting *aiutam! aiutam!* (Help me! Help me!) Panzanello didn't

believe what he heard, requesting that Felice go home – and closed the door.

Squagliacum kept knocking, hollering *Auito! Auito!* Half asleep, Panzanillo

reopened the door, once again listening "a traina isa ina mya garaga".

Impossible, Panzanillo retorted. "Ita cannota bea data a traina isa ina youra

garaga". Believe it or not, it was true.

<u>Buffalo Times</u> and the <u>Italian Il Progresso</u> newspapers reported it

with an article and pictures. "Two box cars jacknifed and smashed into a

garage at the rear of an Exchange Street garage. Forty homes were evacuated

for two hours because of the threat of an explosion of a propane gas tank car

in derailment. Twenty fire department lines were used to wet the car down

before it was towed away".

Our Lady of Perpetual Help did not help the pharmacist's brand

new Packard. Poggerio, the pharmacist, refused to sprinkle salt in the four

corners of his new car. He didn't accept the credibility of the ritualized

seanco (omen). Would you believe Squagliacum's son Umberto's yellow topless, 1927 Chrysler wasn't even scratched. Maybe? — it was a $34.50

miracle or was it because salt was sprinkled in the four corners of his car?

Actually, there was no need to have a car in the neighborhood. Within

walking distance was a Catholic Church, undertaker, grave headstone carver,

barber, beauty shop, dentist, doctor, hospital, shoemaker, bakery, grocery

store, butcher shop, chicken store, fish store, clothing and shoe store. Home

deliveries were made by Felicone's vegetable fruit truck, Richlino the milk

man, Amigones' coal and ice delivery, Melota the fresh fish peddler and

Coola Stuorto the knife sharpener. Even the rag/junkman came with a horse

drawn wagon, shouting Rags! Rags! Rags!

Walking from the neighborhood to downtown, to three "little shows",

Little Hippodrome, Keits or Academy theaters took only 15 minutes. 10 cents

would buy three candy bars. A Baby Ruth, Clark Bar, and Butterfinger at

Sams Drug Store. While viewing the movies, the candy was shared among 3

or 4 kids. Buying candy in the show cost five cents a bar —- too expensive!

For five cents the patrons on Sunday could see a double feature, plus at

least one "B" cowboy picture, cartoons, coming attractions, newsreel, and a

serial. Serials viewers were enticed to return to see what really happened at

the cliff hanger ending of the previous week. Dick Tracy, Frank Buck, The

Wing, Buster Crabb were some of the intriguing serials. Everyone had their own favorite cowboy actors; Bob Steel, Buck Jones, Tom Tyler, Tom Mix, Roy Rogers and others. This complete showing lasted from 1:00 p.m. to 5:00 p.m. Some kids saw it twice and returned home late in the evening.

On Thursday night accompanying the movies, the Academy Show gave free dishes to patrons. Every house in the neighborhood had a complete set of Liberty Bold, warranted 22k gold lined outer rim dishes, made in Japan. Sharing food with neighbors didn't involve returning the dishes. They all used the same dishes.

Nicola, Delorata's nephew, and Big John boarded with the Squagliacum family. Frequently the borders brought Delorta dishes from the Academy Theater. Boarders helped pay the mortgage and other household expenses. Delorata worked very hard. Boarders clothes were washed and pressed. They received their meals, including a packed lunch, placed in pregnant shaped metal black bucket lunch pails. Long submarine shaped sesame covered bread were sliced lengthwise and filled with a variety of food ingredients. Peppers, onions, olive oil were usually accompanied with *salami, capocolla, and frittata.* A bottle of wine and fruit were always in their lunch pails.

Nicola had a bad limp. As a young boy in Acqueviva, Frosolone, while sheparding in the hills, Nicola fell and broke his thigh bone. The leg healed without a cast set by a doctor. It resulted in one leg being shorter.

Nicola and Big John worked paving roads in warm weather. During the winter months they were laid off. Both were eligible for free surplus food. They picked it up with a wagon at the Elk Street market by walking the three mile distance.

Nicola was an alcoholic. Delorata did everything she could to dissuade her nephew from drinking. She shamed him, pleaded with him, and had paesani talk to him. All to no avail. Nicola never stopped drinking. During the week, he controlled himself. He never missed work. Weekends were embarrassingly catastrophic. He visited saloons in the neighborhood, especially Allhands. It was difficult to determine when he wasn't drunk. They took his money without his knowledge. Delorata, pleaded with him to quit, not understanding the illness of alcoholism. Nicola spent two weeks in Alden, New York, where mineral sulphur baths were given. It had no effect. One morning, at the age of 37, Nicola didn't get up for work. Felice went to the boarder's room to awaken him. *"Alzati! Alzati!"* (Get up) itsa tima fora worka". No response! Squagliacum reached over and shook Nicola. He was cold to the touch, eyes closed——- mouth open. He was *morto* (dead)!

Felice told his wife Delorata of her nephew's death. She grieved, cried, trembled and began saying the rosary. Felice Squagliacum walked down Swan Street. Next door to St. Lucy's Church he rang the bell of Sottaterra the funeral director. Signor Sottaterra retrieved the body for embalming.

Nicola's casket was returned to the living room of his Aunt Delorata for viewing. A wreath was placed on the front door. Neighbors knew of the "*morto*" even before the wreath was placed. Nicola was laid out day and night for three days.

Amici (friends) were in and out of the house. Delorata and Felice were never left alone with the corpse. Food was brought in by neighbors. In the living and dining rooms black, kerchiefed women constantly cried. When the black adorned women no longer shed tears, professional mourners took over. Professionals knew their trade and displayed tears. When it was necessary the professionals vehemently cried out "Nicolo youa wera gooda *uomo* (man). Nicola toa younga toa dia". Other mourners joined in with grief and sobs crying out *"E giusto! E giusto!* (It is true, it is true) hea wasa

a gooda man, a gooda man whoa Dio (God) callda toa soona"

In the kitchen men dressed in black arm bands grieved differently.

They told *fatt e scherz* (stories and jokes) including all the virtues of Nicolo.

Coola Stuorto (crooked ass), the local knife sharpener was the center of

story telling. Neighbors went to his house on Myrtle Avenue to pick him up

whenever there was a wake. A wake without *Cool Stuort*, meant *allegrezza*

(happy stories and jokes). Signora Filomena Bue was the only women that sat

with the men in the kitchen sharing stories. Occasionally,

Filomena Bue moved to the living room offering her

black dressed grieving. Espresso topped with anesetta,

made with a Neopolitan *macchinetta* coffee pot was always available to

sustain the all night vigils.

Father Farelli came to the wake three times to lead the rosary.

Afterwards he joined the men in the kitchen. Father's presence necessitated

that dirty stories not be told. While the rosary prayers were said the men

remained quiet.

Funeral mass in black was held at St. Lucy's. Black arm bands, black

dresses were worn by the parishiners. Black vestments were worn by Father

Farelli. Even red- headed Irish Miss Kelly, Father's housekeeper wore black.

Unusual for her. Ordinarily, she wore light colored flowery outfits matching

her bright red hair. Her dresses conformed to her shapely tall thin body.

Neighbors questioned why Miss Kelly never wore a *mandazin*, (apron).

What kind of housekeeper could she be?

Being that there were only a few cars in the neighborhood, plus a

number rented by the undertaker, it meant that each car held a minimum

of 6 adults, with children sitting between their knees. The funeral caravan

traveled for a half hour to Holy Cross *Camposanto* (field of saints) on Ridge

Road, across from Father Baker's Our Lady of Victory Basilica. In addition

to Father Farelli's prayers in Latin, Manoforte gave a eulogy in Italian.

"Nicolo is now in heaven. In many ways he was a

saint. A hard working respectful man. His only minor

vice, was that he was an *briacone*, (a drunk)".

Neighbors continued their condolences, bringing food to Delorata,

her family, including Big John the boarder for the next ten days. Delorata

wore black dresses for years after. Much like other neighbors, after a loved

one died.

During the depression years it was difficult to find work. Delorat's son Umberto and her son in law Eugenio earned money by building and opening an Italian sausage stand in a field at the end of Chicago Street. Umberto asked his father, Squagliacum, if he would clear the high grass and weeds in the field. Squagliacum started sickling the tall weeds. He said "it wasa tooa mucha worka insteada i usda ona smalla matcha toa lighta da grassa ona fira". Dry weeds burned. The wind shifted and the fire burned into high smoking flames, leading toward Di Tondoe's historic restaurant. Firemen were called! Twenty five fire departments came to the rescue. These were the same firemen that prevented Squaqliacum home from blowing up when two box cars containing propane jackknifed and smashed into his garage. The fire was extinguished. Thus saving Di Tondoe's. The most beloved, sacred, historic restaurant on the East Side.

Squagliacum kept insisting at Peppino's that it was only "a smalla matcha". It was God's fault for shifting the wind

Eugenio's little sausage stand was not so small within a few years. It became a full fledged, large windowed, sit- in restaurant. Paesani enjoyed Squagliacum's charcoal grilled home made hot Italian sausage on home made submarine rolls with olive oil, peppers and onions. Squagliacum bought pork butts and clean heavily salted intestine at the William Street stock yards. A hand wound revolving spherical cylinder forced the meat through cutters on which was mounted a long *muttil* (funnel) in front. Long intestines were placed on the funnel. The ground seasoned meat came out into the intestines. Every six inches the intestines were twisted sometimes tied, making links. A good tasty sausage included not only fresh pork butts, with spicies including salt, black pepper, hot red pepper and anise seeds. Filomena Bue's Zinfandel wine, given a superior rating by Gino Stumblucci, was served. West Siders, Love Joyans, East Delavan Italians came, ate, drank and sang Italian songs accompanied by Eugenio piano playing. "O Sole Mio", "O Mama", "O Marie", "Torna a Sorrent", "Santa Lucia", "Vicin U Mare", "Guitarra Romana", and "Mazzolino de Fiore" were sung. Maria Bianca the full fledged West Side 18 year old opera star sang with everyone when she was in Buffalo. Professionally she traveled with the Metropolitan Opera Company.

Every January 17th, St. Anthony Abate festival was held. Paesani went singing from house to house, gathering home made sausage, *prosciutto, supressate*, ending at the Umberto/Eugenio restaurant for singing, sharing and drinking.

At each house, paesani sang the St. Anthony Abate song.

Oche festa oche gioia

Ca' deman e Sant Antuon

Sant Antuon vecchiariell

Ch' la mazza e ru campaniell

O what a feast, O what joy

because tomorrow is St. Anthony's

St. Anthony old man.

With a cane and little bell

Along with merriment, food and joy at Saint Anthony's festival their were also troubles and sorrow.

Lest we leave the reader with a delusion that all things were perfect in this east side Italian neighborhood, we must recount a sad true story.

Big John, a mild mannered gracious generous man lived in Squagliacum's home as a border for six years. Big John was convicted of manslaughter and sent to jail for five years. Why? Blacky, the neighborhood neopolitan bully was always terrorizing neighborhood good people. Blacky picked on women and children, insulting, cursing and ridiculing them. He

picked obscure reasons to challenge and unfairly fight with men. When he

insulted, shoved, and cursed Big John, it became his last and final encounter.

Big John walked home, retrieved Squagliacum's 16

gage, double barrel shotgun, loaded it with two buck shot

shells and walked back with the gun pointed down at his

side.

Blacky got his name, because of his dark skin, unshaven face and

evil black soul. Blacky hung out at the corner of Myrtle Avenue and Seneca

Place in front of Mangione's delicatessen. Blacky was cursing people across

the street. Nobody wanted to walk by him. Rather they crossed the street,

avoiding him. Blacky was drunk with his infamous power laughing as

people avoided him. He turned. Big John, a few feet away had his shotgun

pointed. In a fraction of a second, Blacky turned white. His eyes and mouth

wide open, his brain perceiving what was about to happen. Triggers were

pulled. Bam! Bam! Steel round pellets pierced Blacky's torso, seeping

through his shirt and into his hairy chest. Blood came squirting out. The

blast backed his body through Mangione's plate glass window. Amici, in the neighborhood realized what happened. They did not grieve. They were pleased with Blacky's death.

Big John walked to Police Precinct #2 on south Division near Spring Street and turned himself in by surrendering the shotgun. At his trial many many neighbors testified as to the goodness of Big John and the ugliness of Blacky. Big John's Irish defense lawyer, recommended by Sarto, was able to reduce a seven year term to five years. Because of good behavior, Big John was out in three years. Squagliacum with his organetto and friends greeted Big John upon his release from incarceration. Neighbors held a party at Umberto/Eugenio's restaurant.

Blacky had no wake or funeral. No one wished to grieve and cry for him. Neighbors said *"a fat la morte di un cane"* (he died like a dog that he was). His pine box burial at the outer edges of Pine Ridge Cemetery had a small ground imbedded stone with a number on it. Not even a name!

Chapter 8

Filomena Bue

(The Ox)

"Da Na Botta" Filomena. Filomena a wide shouldered women power- pushed the wine press pipe causing wine to flow out of the almost dry mash of concord grapes. Manoforte winked at his son Angelo not to give a shot to the pipe thus allowing Filomena to do all of the pushing and pressing. Filomena could easily power push by herself. Wine was being pressed in Filomena's cellar. Norwegian adults would have to bow down in her low ceiling cellar. Men and women in the neighborhood could easily walk straight up and have room to spare.

Filomena broke the rules of the neighborhood Italian culture. She was slightly taller than her *"Mush Mush"* thin, unassuming, soft spoken husband Orlando, nicknamed "Scuscabiell". To hide her height, so not to cause neighborhood gossip, she never wore high heeled shoes. She always wore her long bunned black hair flat on her head. Her height was seldom, if ever noticed. Filomena lied to neighbors saying she was one year younger, than her husband. Actually, being 35 days older than *"Scuscabiell"*. Thus following the rules, that women needed to be shorter and younger than their husbands. Weighing more, no matter how much more than their husbands had no cultural relevance. There was also an anatomical physical difference between Filomena and Orlando. Filomena was stronger because of her wide shoulders and narrow hips. Orlando was thin, narrow shouldered and his hips were as wide at Filomena's shoulders. No other neighborhood family had these unusual physical characteristics. Therefore no cultural rules had developed for wide hipped men, nor broad shouldered women.

Scuscabiell worked at the Elk Street market. His family supplemented his income by selling wine at twenty-five cents per gallon. Twelve 50 gallon oak barrels were stored in their stone walled damp cellar. Eventually, Filomena Bue, which literally translates to Filomena Ox, learned that it would be more profitable to sell moonshine. The family eventually graduated upward, selling alcohol for thirty-five cent per pint. This enterprising venture could only be entered into with utmost secrecy. Why? While they were in the wine selling business Orlando told his taller, stronger, broad- shouldered wife not to sell wine to anyone unknown to the family. What happened? A gentleman, *bestia* really, dressed in unpressed wrinkled shirt, pin stripped jacket and bib overalls smoking a DiNobile cigar. He presented himself as a local *uomo* (man). His sartorial appearance, DiNobile cigar smoking, gentle Italian speech, was not unlike other men in the neighborhood.. Filomena was persuaded to sell him a gallon of foxy tasting concord wine for fifty cents. Happily, Filomena made an extra twenty-five cents, doubling the usual cost of a gallon. She was doomed! Filomena was arrested by this disguised *"bestia, sonvabitcha"* government treasury agent. Orlando heard of the miserable event through the immediate neighborhood gossip system. Leaving work, he rushed home. Filomena was going to jail. Scuscabiell was not able to persuade the *"bestia sonnabitcha"* treasury agent to substitute him for his arrested wife. Filomena needed to stay home to care for their eight children. An exaggerated number. They only had four. Orlando spoke slowly in his best broken English dialect. There was no convincing the *Merd D Cane* (dog shit) agent.

Raffaela, age 14, took over household duties while her mother was in jail. All neighborhood girls learned housekeeping which included cooking, baking, and sewing! How to *sparagna* (save) when buying anything was taught by mothers. Every day, except Sundays, Raffaela waited for Filachone, the fruit and vegetable huckster, to come by with his truck. This really was a social event. Signora, e Signorina came out of their houses to buy and gossip. When Raffaela went to Mangiones store down the street, she needed no money. Mangione and other stores put it "on the books". Families had book pages assigned to them. Clerks penciled in what was bought and the cost. Families paid the book bill when they had money. Some paid by the week. Others by the month. Families undergoing difficulties took a longer period of time. The "book" was never cheated, always paid by families.

Mr. Richlino delivered three quarts of milk to Bue family six days a week. Once or twice a week Signor Melota, the fish peddler, pushed his wagon down the street shouting *Pesce Viva! Pesce Viva!* (Live fish! Live fish!) Signor Melota, when he realized family hardships added extra fish at no cost.

The three boys in the Bue family were responsible for helping make and retrieve wine as needed. They went with their parents by street car, to the Bailey Clinton market to buy boxes of California grapes, Zinfandel, Alicanti, and Muscatel from Mr.

Deziderio, whose truck delivered the grape filled boxes to their home. Crossing Clinton Street, the Bue family went to the farmers market to buy local purple Concord and white Niagara grapes.

Mr. Amigone delivered coal with his truck, dumping it at the curb side. Filomena's sons carried the coal down the cellar in bushels. Once the burned ashes were removed from the kitchen side by side cooking stove and the pot bellied cast iron dining room stove. Ashes were taken out to the vegetable garden. The lower portion of the barrel shaped dining room stove was so hot that the cast iron turned flame red. Considering this, one would surmise that the entire house would be warm. But it wasn't so. Bedrooms were cold. Winter mornings, it was not unusual to awaken to windows that were opaque with covered ice.

Mr. Amigone also delivered ice for home ice boxes. Front windows portrayed a rotating sign which indicated that he deliver 25 pounds, 50 pounds, 75 pounds or a 100 pounds of ice. Mr. Amigone had a rubber tarp over his right shoulder when he carried the tonged ice. There were times when Amigone walked three flights of stairs carrying 100 pounds of ice. No ————this was not easy but necessary to make a living.

Some families sent their sons with a wagon to pick up ice at Mook's

Ice and Service Corporation, which manufactured ice at 419 North Division

Street. It was cheaper than having ice delivered.

INCARCERATION

Filomena was incarcerated for ten days in the Erie County Franklin

Street Jail. Every day, Scuscabiell with his three sons and daughter walked

to see Filomena through the barred second floor window. Their mother

was not aggravated, upset, or depressed. She hollered out with *allegrezza*

(happiness) that *"Questa e na bella vacanza"* (This is a beautiful vacation).

She didn't have to wash clothes, prepare lunches, wash floors, sew or cook

dinner. She rested when she wished. Police matrons fed her *Medegon* food

including sliced white bread. Filomena missed *verza, pasta e fasool, pasta*

e polpette, vino (greens, pasta and beans, spaghetti and meat balls, wine)

and most of all the sesame covered crusty Italian home made bread baked

at Mangano's Bakery.

Ten days later, 19 of her Myrtle Avenue neighbors greeted her release

from jail. Squagliacum  played the Organeto

accompanied by Veto Bue on his mandolin.

Greeters shared their fresh baked pizza, as they walked the Bue family home. The party continued with wine drinking and singing.

Now the reader understands why severe secure secrecy was necessary for the Bue's family graduation into making still alcohol.

Filomena was the only woman allowed to play Morra, Bocce, Briscola card games with the Amici from Peppino's. She could *bestemmia* (swear, curse) and drink as well as any man. Held in high respect, there never was any sexual intimation toward her. After all, she was as strong as most of the men.

The reader may recall that Peppino did not allow card or *morra* playing in his shop. However, it was not unusual for people in the neighborhood to play *morra* on street corners, backyards and at parties. The game was alluring for it required no cards or bocce balls. It only required the 5 fingers of one hand.

The object of *morra* is to guess the total number of fingers extended by opponents. At the same moment two players, face to face, throw out one or more fingers of one hand, simultaneously shouting out the number of exposed fingers. Zero is throwing out a closed fist. *Tuta la morra* is the extension of five fingers; predicting that the other player will also throw out five fingers. Ten fingers extended is *tuta la morra*.

A predetermined number of rounds determines a match. Usually a round is won with three points. Then the round winner proceeds to the next opponent. Play continues until one player or one team reaches the number of rounds previously decided upon to win the match.

An *amici* team consisting of Peppino, Manoforte, Panzanillo, Stumblucci played against the team of Filomena Bue, Sarto, Un'occhio and Squagliacum. Team members varied every time the *morra* game was played.

Filomena Bue was unique in her play. Most often she beat the men. Was she para psychic? Could she read opponents body language before fingers were thrown? It was never understood — never learned — never known.

She consecutively beat Peppino, Manoforte, Panzanillo and Stumblucci with three point rounds. Filomena arrived at 12 points defeating the four player opponent team, allowing them only five points. When this happened, other team players made a line up change placing Filomena last. Without this alteration, other team members would never have the opportunity to play the game.

Peppino explained that the ancient Egyptian sculptors played a game of this type. It was also played by the Romans, who called it *Micare Digitus*, or finger flashing. The game is known to the Chinese and various island tribes in the Pacific. *Morra* is especially played in Italy, other parts of Europe, Northern Africa and Abyssinia.

Filomena was *analfabeta* (illiterate). San Fele, in the province of Potenza, in the region of Basilicata was her birth place. Her distinction! She was the paesani of Signor Sottaterra the undertaker. Mr. Sottaterra was handsome, and spoke perfect English.

Filomena's Upbringing

Filomena talked with her family as they sat around the dinner table. She described how she tended sheep in the hills of San Fele during the day. When she returned at dusk, she rushed to the local dressmaker Zia Olivia to observe and help Zia make other clothes and dresses for towns people. Zia Olivia was a natural sartorial designer, skilled and able to make corduroy suits for *contadino* (peasant) farmers. Amateurishly, Filomena learned the dressmaking process. When she migrated to America at the age of 18, she naturally brought her dressmaking skills with her. Few neighbor were aware of her sewing abilities and were amazed that her children and grandchildren were dressed in expensive latest fashions. No one else had the money to pay for these exciting well fitting clothes. Her secret. Filomena walked uptown, which only took 15 minutes and bought the most expensive dresses, coats and accessories from J N Adams department store. Escalator rides were taken to the fourth floor clothing department. Returning home, she unstitched the clothing and proceeded to make patterns with newspapers. When completed she resewed the clothing and returned them to JN Adams for refunds. These patterns were kept in empty macaroni boxes. Filomena could estimate how much cloth to buy at the discounted, garlically smelling, Olga's haberdashery located a few block away at Swan and South Cedar Street.

Parishioners were open mouthed, astounded as Signora Bue walked into St. Lucy's Church for Easter Mass accompanied by nine grandchildren. Six Signorine, black eyed with long Shirley Temple style curled chestnut hair. They wore various colors and designs of velvet dresses. Three boys wore *Nonna's* (grandma's) hand sewn wool jackets, pants, shirts and ties.

They carried bought hats which grandma could not make. Zia Olivia never taught Filomena how to make men's hats.

HOUSE ON FIRE

While Filomena was sewing a fire started in the second floor of the Bue's two family brick home. Vito, Bue's son, ran across the street and pulled the fire alarm system. Hook and ladder #8 located on Chicago and South Park, and Pumper #12 a block and a half away were alerted. Hook and ladder axed a hole in the roof releasing gasses and smoke, preventing back drafts when second floor windows were broken. Pumper #12 watered the second floor. Other firemen had rushed into the first floor throwing canvas protective tarps over the furniture. Seeping water from the quickly controlled fire, was minimized. The cause of the fire was never learned. *Grazia a Dio* (thank God) no one was hurt. Gino Stumblucci, was called in and made repairs to the axed roof.

Scuscabiell, his three sons, daughter and Filomena, who knew how to sew, were not carpenters. They decided to save money by making their own repairs, not heeding the proverb *chi sparagna spreca* (he who tries to save really wastes). It took them two months to make half assed repairs. How mixed up were the fixings? The floor in the kitchen was uneven, slanting measurable to one side. Eating on the kitchen table was an arduous Olympic event, when Bifulcos truck sped by Bue's house. The truck caused vibrations and made dishes of food slide from end to end of the table. Spaghetti sauce with meatballs readily mixed. Eating had to be swift or uncontrolled dishes slid off the table onto the slanted floor. Wine, red tomato sauce, rolling meat balls became entwined with spaghetti putting Jackson Pollock's abstract paintings to shame.

The reader may assume that the blunder of slanted floors was the worse half assed rebuilding tragedy. But it wasn't! Difficult to understand, the Bue family completed their work but forgot the essence of a livable home. They forgot to create a room for a toilet. Their pride in rebuilding without the help of professional carpenters suddenly regressed the family into depression and self anger. Anger, they in voice and body communicated. As they faced each other they bit their index and middle fingers, for forgetting to build the "God Dammed toilet". Peppino, learning of the catastrophe, repeated many times *"chi sparagna spreca"* (he who tries to save really wastes).

After all, the Bue family couldn't permit their upstairs tenants to use their first floor *baccausa* especially in the middle of the night. Also, they realized that tenants would not walk five blocks to the public bathrooms at Benneth Park, across from Tech High School, either day or night.

Their only remaining solution was to again call Gino Stumblucci the plumber and handy man, who had already repaired their axed roof. The money they saved and additional funds were needed to pay Gino Stumblucci. Gino investigated and decided that the toilet could only be placed above the last three steps of the stairs going from the first to the second floor. There was no other space available.

When the work was done, adults climbing the three stairs had to lower their heads or bang heads on the ceiling. The strategy for using the toilet was to walk up the three stairs backwards placing your butt on the toilet first dropping pants and bloomers. The method required kenisolgic athletic abilities. Slowly, meticulously you had to hold your pants or bloomers above the ankles to prevent tripping and falling. Then you slowly walked backwards one step at a time.

Another method, involved lowering pants and bloomers below the knees and gingerly walking head lowered, up three steps, then nimbly turned your fanny on the toilet seat. *Gente* (people) using the toilet described it at as podium and said "da wera gonna maka a speacha". Bue's *baccausa* (toilet) became known as the speech center of the neighborhood.

After making a speech, the kitchen sink was used to wash up. Luckily the three stair *baccausa* had a slanted door to fit the crooked walls. Because the door didn't fit well, like everything else on the second floor, light from the living room gave direction to the use of the speach room.

Neighbors on Myrtle Avenue, in fact the entire neighborhood, had no telephones nor did they need them. By simply opening windows next door neighbors could gossip. It was not difficult to talk with neighbors across the street. Shouting communicated messages. Their was a common way of conveying messages window to open window. Messages were easily and efficiently returned. Down stairs and upstairs tenants had a code for reaching each other banging a spoon on extruded water pipes. One bang meant *buon giorno* (good morning), hope everything is well. Two bangs meant come up or down so we can *parla* (talk). Three bangs meant an emergency, rush!

As Filomena walked down her sidewalk alleyway to get to her back door, she smelled urine. At first she didn't believe her nasal senses. How could this be she thought? Within a week the odor of urine became more pronounced. Filomena became aware that the alleyway below her neighbors

window, was moist and heavily scented. Arising early, she investigated what

was happening under the window. Now the truth was revealed. Johnny, the

17 year-old boy next door was pissing out of the raised window. Filomena

stratagised a plan. The next morning with a broom in hand she waited for

Johnny to repeat his morning ritual. As the teenager was pissing, Bang!

Felomena hit the boys groin with the straw end of the broom. Johnny

screamed in pain. Needless to say, Johnny never peed out the window again.

At Peppino's, the laughable event was common talk. The nickname ascribed

was *La Famiglia di Pisciasotto* (the family that pees their pants).

When Johnny became draft age, he was notified to appear for his

physical. He appeared smelling like shit. No one wanted to be near him.

Johnny told the doctors that he had no control of his bowel movements. The

army told him to go home as "4F", physically unfit. Johnny was happy, for

he fooled the army physicians. Wait a while. The recruiting personnel were

not convinced and began visiting Johnny *pisciasotto* at home. Realizing that

visits would be made, John took no chances always shitting his pants. His

family and friends didn't want to be near him. He could not hold a job. He

was isolated.

At Peppino's, amici discussed Johnny in dialect saying *"P non i alla guerra se cacat entr l calz"* (he shit in his socks so he would not go to war).

Johnny finally gave up! His strategy caused self inflicted loneliness. He went to the Marine recruiting station, passed the physical without a stink, becoming a volunteer.

Johnny was sent to the South Pacific and made initial landings at Guadalcanal, Tarawa, Midway and Okinawa. These frightening landings and ensuing battles gave him valid reasons for shitting his pants. But!— — he never did. His families *sopra nome* (nickname) was expanded to *la familiga di piscia caca sotto* (peeing and shitting their pants family).

Filomena's graduation from selling wine to producing alcohol took time to plan and investment. Eventually, the Bue family decided to attach a block building to their house, thus giving the necessary space to hold a still and barrels of mash. Felomena hired Manoforte to construct the still building. The Bue family experience in their half assed fixing of the second floor was not to be repeated. Manoforte, the stone mason from the hamlet of Callecarrisa, Frosolone, accepted the job.

Hod and block carrier, *briacone* Alchi worked for Allhands saloon as a night maintence man, which really meant that Alchi washed floors, took out garbage and cleaned whatever was necessary. Being an alcoholic, Alci received pay from Allhands saloon in the form of whiskey. Alchi showed up the first day to carry hod and blocks. He was slow, unsteady, awkward and never showed up the second day. Filomena substituted for Alchi from then on. Although she was broad shouldered, strong, had calloused hands, she was not as powerful as Manoforte. Actually, the moonshine building was completed much sooner than anticipated. Filomena carried three blocks at a time, where as most hod carrying men could only carry two. She carried one in each hand, plus a third on her head. She needed no rest, working from morning until night. Signora Bue was the best hod and block carrier that ever assisted Manoforte. In a pinch, she would help Manoforte but wouldn't accept permanent employment. She needed time to manage her moonshine business and time to sew for her grandchildren. Everyone in the neighborhood knew why Felomena constructed the building. They would never squeal to the *"bestia* government treasury controllers"*. The Bue family was making an honest living. Anyway, Father Ferelli said "It was not a sin to make and sell alcohol. If one got caught, it was a problem".

Filomena and family moved all their 50 gallon oak barrels from the cellar into the block building, which by the way had no windows and just one door. To buy an alcoholic  still, Filomena went to Mr. Salvotucci, *ru stagnar* (tinsmith) housed at 338 swan Street. Signor Salvotucci learned his craft in Italy. He made pots, pans, water jugs, cake and bread pans from copper, tin and brass. Obviously there was no need for his copper making pots and pans in Buffalo, NY. Did his skill go to waste? No!! In fact, he became wealthy making alcoholic copper stills for moonshine entrepreneurs. He received clandestine orders from Western New York and from other parts of the country.

Bue family members had their tasks. There was not to be a repeat of past circumstances, when Mama Bue spent ten days in jail. Selling alcohol was governed by rigorous laws. Getting caught now meant years not days in jail as had once happened for selling wine. One son, Silvano, was designated to place burlap bags over nearby manholes, preventing alcohol odor from escaping into the air.

During spring, summer, and fall all things went well. Money was coming in heavily. Bue family was proud for they beat the *"sonvabitchi besta"* government treasury agents. What happened? Silvano preferred being with his teenage friends instead of covering manholes with burlap. Alcohol could now be smelled. *"Bestia"* treasury men began to smell it as well, but could not pinpoint where the odor came from. Snow fell. All roofs were snow covered but the block building was abnormally dry. Why? Mash brewing generated heat, flowing up, melting snow on the roof. "Bestia" were now sure where the alcohol was being stilled. Smell, and no snow on the roof brought the treasury men to Bue's block building.

Scuscabiell was arrested. Filomena went to Sarto for a lawyer recommendation. Sarto made suits, coats for municipal dignitaries, police and lawyers.

At the trial the Bue family's defense at trial was that the building was rented. They had nothing to do with the 13 barrels of mash and the still. Obviously, this was a poor excuse. *Scuscabiell* went to jail for one year. Filomena, retreated from making moonshine and returned to selling wine. She went to work full time as a hod block carrier for Manoforte, while her husband served time. The entire neighborhood, including *Medegons,* *repeated that the* "besta" prohibition treasury agents were wrong for arresting and convicting *Scuscabiell*. He was making an honest living supporting his family and not receiving welfare help during the depression.

Filomena's family was helped by neighbors from all over the East Side. They bought wine from her, even though they all had 50 gallon barrels in their cellars.

I need not repeat this again, but you guessed it! When Scuscabiell was released, after eight months for good behavior, the *paesani* greeted him with a party. Squagliacum played the organetto, Vito, their son, played mandolin with Felomena playing cords on her guitar. The block building did not go to waste. Windows were put in by volunteers Manoforte and Squagliacum. They were assisted by hod carrier Filomena.

Selling wine and Scuscabiell's work at Elks market slowly proved profitable. The Bue children and later the grandchildren attended St. Lucy's Catholic School. Vito, their genius musician son, played any string

 The Juilliard School

instrument from mandolin to harp. Vito received a full scholarship from the Julliard Music School in New York City. *Amici* (friends), at Peppino's, all agreed that Veto was an excellent musician and deserved the scholarship,

but they all decided that the intercession of St.
Cecelia, patron saint of music helped. A large icon of
St. Cecelia with votive lamps adorned Bue's dining
room. In addition, there were crucifixes in every
room including the attic, cellar and Manoforte's block
alcohol making building.

Vito earned a bachelor of music degree in orchestral
instruments, specializing in guitar. His room and board was
paid by the money he earned playing jazz gigs. Every couple
of weeks, Filomena mailed food boxes to her son. Boxes
containing *caciocavallo*, homemade dried *linguine*, *parmigiano* chunks of
grating cheese, fried crisp meatballs and homemade bottled sauce.

Upon completion of his degree, Vito returned
home, playing double base with the Buffalo Philharmonic
Orchestra. Paul Whitman invited him to travel on the road
with his big band. Vito remained in Buffalo playing with
combos, and sat in when big bands came to the uptown
"Big Shows" Shea's Buffalo and Century theaters. For twenty-five cents,
not only was a top rated movie provided but often a big band was included.

Bands such as, Tommy and Jimmy Dorsey, Cab Caloway, Count Bassie, Woodie Herman and their singers Frank Sinatra, Ray and Bob Eberly and Ella Fitzgerald.

Squagliacum's organetto, signora Bue's guitar cord playing was accompanied by Vito's mandolin playing at parties held in the neighborhood. Filomena and Scuscabiell sat back with immense pride as their children and grandchildren successfully grew into first generation Italian Americans.

Even though they struggled in their first years in Buffalo, they were glad that they left San Fele. If they remained in Italy, they probably would still be tending sheep in the Appenine Mountains. In the United States opportunity was offered. Working hard, their *famiglia* prospered.

Chapter 9

Mr. Georgio and Peppino

Peppino Mirca learned the shoemaking trade as an apprentice, beginning at the age 6 and continuing to age 12, in the small village of Acqueviva Collecroce, Campobasso in the Appenine Mountains of Abruzzi. He was an altar boy, and his  pastor recognized Peppino's intelligence and tutored him for 15 minutes every day after Mass. The pastor persuaded Peppino's parents that their son was spiritual, bright and should attend the Trivento seminary for the priesthood. The local priest made all of the necessary arrangements.

Trivento seminary, which also housed the seat of the bishop for Souther Abruzzi referred to as Molise, was about 30 kilometers from Peppino's home. Traveling by carriage that would go around the Appenine mountain roads cost money. Peppino used this route to get home for his Christmas vacation. This two hour ride went through the towns of Monte

Falcone nel Sannio and Roccavino. During warm weather, Peppino chose to ride his donkey *Cannone* (Cannon), on dirt paths over the Appenine Mountains to Trivento. This route took about three hours. The only cost was feed for his donkey. Ordinarily Peppino went home to Acqueviva Colla croce, three times per year.

Until the age of 21, Peppino studied at the seminary, learning Cannon law, Greek, Latin, and Tuscan formal Italian as well as other priestly studies.

Italy entered the first world war on May 23, 1915, resulting in Peppino being drafted. As a seminarian, a deferment would have been achievable, but Peppino did not apply. After following basic training he was sent to the battles of Isongo which lasted from 1915 to 1917. The morale of the troops was kept high by a marching band that played military marches, which included two songs that had deep meaning for all of Italy: *Inno Di Mameli* music by M. Novaro with words by Goffaedo Mameli. The last stanza was of particular sensitivity to soldiers in Italian:

Son giunchi che piegano

Le spade vendute:

Gia l'Aquila d'Austria

Le penne ha perdute

Il sangue d'Italia

E il sangue polacco

Beve col Cosacco

Ma il cor le brucia

Stringiamoci a coorte

Siam pronti alla morte;

Italia chiamo!

Translated to English:

Mercenary swords

are feeble reeds.

And the Austrian eagle

Has lost his plumes

This eagle that drank the blood

of Italy and Poland

together with the Cossack

But this has burned his gut.

Let us gather in legions.

Ready to die!

Italy has called

From Giuseppe Verdi's opera Nabucco, soldiers sang along with the military marching band. In groups, soldiers also sang a'capello the Hebrew Slave chorus. This disguised song concomitantly encouraged the Italians to rise up against their Austrian subjugators.

These battles were fought along the Isongo River on the eastern section of the Italian front. Twelve battles took place at Isongo. Following the eleventh battle around Gorizia, the Austro-Hungarian front was in jeopardy of collapse. The Germans were sent to provide help to their Austro-Hungarian allies. Referred to as the "Battle of Caporetto," the 12th battle of Isongo was launched at 2:00 A.M. on October 1917. Heavy artillery barrages of high explosives initiated the battle. Peppino, who withstood the first 11 battles, was not fortunate in the 12th. Shrapnel pierced his helmet and destroyed a portion of his skull bone. Five days later, he awakened in a military hospital with heavy bandages encircling his head. *Infermiera* (nurses) explained that he was very *"fortunato"* (lucky). A thin stainless steel plate was placed over the destroyed bone, meticulously covered with stretched head skin and sutured. To cover the scars, Peppino let his hair grow longer, changed his hair style, combing it from the right to left. Previously, he combed his hair in the common way from left to right.

Infrequently he would get stinging, massive headaches. When these headaches occurred he required immediate silence and needed to be by himself. Peppino became devoted to St. Theresa of Avila, the patron saint of headache suffers. In addition, he admired St. Theresa for her scholarly work having become one of two women named as a "Doctor of the Church". Peppino, while at the seminary had read two of her books "Interior Castle" and "Why of Perfection" in Latin.

Later he learned that the "Battle of Caporetto" was lost due to the poor leadership of General Luigi Cardonna. Italians suffered 300,000 casualties, *"fortunatamente"* (fortunately) 90% were taken as prisoners.

Peppino returned home to the heart of Abruzzi, to the soul of Slavic residents, Acqueviva Collecroce. No longer able to attend the seminary, Peppino worked at his *calzolaio* (shoemaker trade),

In the later part of the 1400's, Turks invaded Yugoslavia. Many

Serbo Croates escaped by sailing across the Adriatic and migrating to

Abruzzi. Three Slavic enclaves established themselves in Abruzzi, one being

Acqueviva Collecroce. Many of these Slavic people were noted for their

red hair, freckles and ability to learn languages. These Slavic Italian towns

carried on with their cultural traditions. Acqueviva Collecroce was well

known throughout Abruzzi for its delicious preparation of pork imbedded

with paprika.

Peppino did not have red hair or freckles but had an ease in learning

languages. He spoke Slave, dialect Italian as well as Tuscan Italian, Greek,

Latin and English.

Within one year following his discharge from the army, he married

a neighbor, named Bianchini. Peppino and pregnant Bianchini migrated to

the U.S. with the intent of settling in Buffalo, New York, where a number

of paesani had established themselves. When they left their hometown, the

population was reduced from 2223 to 2221.

In Buffalo, the Peppino Mirca family had four children, one of

whom, Berto studied at the Paolist Fathers seminary and became an order priest. Berto, had the ability to write pamphlets, magazine articles, books of

faith. The Paolist Order was known for publishing religious material.

Not surprisingly, Biachini never learned English. At home they

spoke Slav. Within the neighborhood, almost everyone spoke Italian. There

was no need to learn English. Their four children spoke English, Slav and

the Abruzzese Italian dialect. He named his one daughter Theresa, after his

patron saint, Theresa of Avila.

Peppino went home for lunch most of the year. Although he lived on

South Division near Pine Street, he walked home in a round about way. Down

Chestnut Street, passing South Division and then turning right onto North

Division. Here he met Mr. Georgio and gave him a carob stick, comfortably

talking with him for a few minutes then caressing Mr. Georgio's face with

his finger tips. Then he proceeded to walk home. This ritual was repeated

at 6:00 p.m. when Peppino finished with his shoe shop work. Mr. Georgio

always waited for the carob stick, soft consoling voice, and compassionate

feel of Peppino's facial fingertip caress. This made Mr. Georgio relaxed,

accepted and happy.

During the warm weather months Mr. Georgio was carried down

from his second story flat by either his older brother, Orlando, or Bucky

Zacarella, a golden gloves champion, who lived on the third floor. Mr.

Georgio was carried down about 7:00 A.M. when his protective brother

and Bucky left for work at the Lafayette Hotel. At 7:00 P.M. in the evening,

when returning from work, they carried Mr. Georgio to the second floor.

During the winter month, Mr. Georgio remained in his flat with his black

dressed guilt ridden depressed mother. Her son, Georgio was born crippled.

The whereabouts of his father was unknown. Maybe he returned to Italy,

or according to the other rumor, Georgio's father ran away with the New

Orleans *puttana* (whore) strip teaser who worked at the Allhands Saloon

and Night Cub. Even during the winter months, Peppino visited Mr. Georgio

twice per day and once on Sunday.

Mr. Georgio was confined to a woven caned, high back, wheel chair.

Georgio's heavy black beard, was shaven daily by his mother. His thick head

of hair was also kept shaved. This made it easier for his mother to manage

and wash her son's head. Mr. Georgio's eyes were large, black, within a

long, thin, high cheeked face revealing a prominent hooked nose and thin

lips. When alert, Mr. Georgio tried to sit up straight. His left arm held close

to his body was bent at the elbow. His wrist was bent upwards with fingers

and thumb clutched together covering the palm of his hand. His right arm was not crippled. Mr. Georgio's legs were as thin as the rest of his body. His

right leg and knee overlapped his left knee. Both of his deformed lower legs

always pointed downwards. His right foot was positioned on top of his left

foot. Georgio's feet were not able to bend upwards. He wore ankle length,

soft black leather shoes which covered his deformed feet. Manoforte's six

year old grandson once described Mr. Georgio's feet as looking

like the feet of Jesus on the cross. Mr. Georgio's voice was

limited to groans. He grunted when angry. Spittle constantly

dribbled down the corners of his lips. He wiped the spittle, as best he could

with his right shoulder and arm. His eyes glistened, and he eagerly smiled

when given attention. When ignored Mr. Georgio slumped to his left in a

sitting fetal position.

On the sidewalk, he could haphazardly manipulate his wheelchair

with his right arm. Ambulating slowly he moved from his house to either

corner of the block, preferring to stand in front of Narone's Saloon next to a

narrow alleyway. The alleyway led from North Division and wound around

to Chestnut Street. Neighborhood people reacted differently to Mr. Georgio.

It was obvious that some, mostly adults would avoid him completely by

crossing to the other side of the street. A few other *Cristiani* walked by paying their respects. Little children were awed and puzzled. They stared not certain how to respond.

Some older kids and teenagers taunted and teased him. Mr. Georgio interacted by grunting, biting his right index and middle fingers in a gesture of anger. He attempted to spit at them. As rapidly as he became angry Georgio broke into an accepting warm smile if his taunters smiled.

Bucky, not being discourteous and without malice, would say of his friend Georgio, "He is like a puppy. No matter how you mistreat Georgio, he will accept you if you let him."

Angelo was on Thanksgiving vacation from school and went to visit Peppino. From Thanksgiving to Christmas, Peppino carried a brown bag lunch to his shop. Peppino closed the store during his lunch hour, eating and working alone in the backroom. *"Come sta"* (How are you) Angelo? "Eata *pranzo* (lunch) widda mia." Peppino was cutting a piece of ox blood, patent leather on his bench as he was eating lunch.

Respectfully, Angelo addressed Peppino as Zio (uncle)"How is your family?" "Everything isa fine, Angelo anda howa are youa doing ata da universsida?" They continued their conversation. Angelo then asked about Georgio.

What followed completely engrossed Angelo and was more profound, then any philosophy or other courses that he had been studying at St. Louis University Graduate School of Social Work. From his seminary days, trained in scholastic philosophy and theology. Peppino referred to Mr. Georgio. Peppino dropped his Abruzzese dialect and spoke in Tuscan Italian.

"Angelo, people look upon Mr. Georgio with pity, disdain or make him into a saint. When he dies, he will directly experience the beatific vision. This may or may not be true, only God knows. Many of us treat him like a youngster, a kid, not a man, 26 years old. He is deserving of being called "Mr. Georgio"

"Angelo, the neighborhood thinks of me as a saint because I visit Mr. Georgio everyday. I visit Mr. Georgio because my humanity is fulfilled. When you are with him there is no pretense. Mr. Georgio is like bread and wine. His distorted body, with spittle running down the sides of his mouth is what people see; they don't look deeper. Mr. Georgio greets people with complete openness. He neither questions not defends. When ridiculed, he hurts and fights back, but! will immediately forgive at the slightest sign of acceptance. His accepting spirit can be seen in his eyes His spirit is clear as glistening white wine. Mr. Georgio does not relate to time, place, or circumstance. He loves freely and openly. He gives not in the way the world expects nor wants. Because of his unconditional accepting behavior, he frightens many of us.

Let me say the universe is so enormous and at one and the same time so minute that the most sophisticated telescopes and microscopes will never expose limits. These limits are mysteries: mysteries, that we will infinitely explore. We are amazed at these propositions. Yet, we fail to understand Mr. Georgio's wonderment of personhood. He is unique like you and me. There was and never will be another Mr. Georgio. He thinks, he feels, he reacts with simplicity. He may not as sophisticated or as muddled as many of us. We are always worried about the world around us, how we will be perceived. Mr. Georgio is pure and direct in his behaviors. His actions are creative like all of our reactions. He smiles, mumbles, raises his arm, these are all decisions, leading to creative acts. They occur once in their own way never to be repeated again, like all out actions. The world does not define his actions as creative. He will not be singled out in museums or receive honors because of his intellectual abilities. Nevertheless, in relation to the totality of the universe, in its vastness and minuteness, his actions are creative, unique. Mr. Georgio knows the essence of life. He wants to be sociable. He

needs people to know he exists. When this happens he sits up in his chair

and rewards us with his loving smile. His look is a pure uncluttered, smile

of acceptance. His smile rises from the debt of his soul. It is a smile of joy.

His accepting spiritual smile puts our smiles to shame.

"It becomes our problem when we don't take time to witness the

beauty in him. We have taken on the values of the world which emphasize

that when persons cannot function within our economic order, they have

no worth, no status, no prestige, no meaning. We are the ones that are truly

crippled. Many of us do not explore or exercise the inner essence of our

being. We grade ourselves by the rules of the world. When caught in this

value system we are the —- losers! Mr. Georgio responds right now, to

goodness, returning it without qualification. If you think about it Angelo,

Mr. Georgio is more like us than unlike us. He thinks!——— Though

limited by world standards, He feels!——— He acts!——— He has skin,

blood, hair, eyes like all of us. He may not be perfect as we would like him

to be. He is a mystery!

"It would appear as if the aura of ideas was left out of Mr. Georgio's

being, but —— his spirit remains whole. To God, Mr. Giorgio is as creative, as famous, as prestigious as any world defined genius. God has allowed Mr. Georgio to be shared with us. Unfortunately, many of us do not take time to suffer through the initial abhorrence of witnessing beyond his tortured body and see a radiant glaring glistening soul".

Angelo remained quiet and pensive for many days following his visit with Peppino. Angelo meditated on the realities that he didn't want to admit.

THEN IT HAPPENED! – during the fall wine making season! Gossip spread like the ubiquitous neighborhood smell of mash.

Georgio was lost! Bucky and Georgio's older brother, Orlando searched all night. Neighborhood adults and children searched in and outside the neighborhood. All the way to Broadway, Main Street, Jefferson Avenue and as far as the Pennsylvania Central Railroad tracks paralleling Scott Street. Mr. Georgio was not found! Not found!

Rumors were that the bums living in the lodging house on Michigan Avenue abducted Mr. Georgio. Others said, it must be the Irish gang from the other side of the Chicago Street bridge. The gang must have hurt Mr. Georgio, in retaliation for Italian boys dating redheaded and blond Irish girls from the first ward. None of these rumors made sense, but were spread through open windows and neighbors sitting on stoops licking ice cream. Tenement buildings had their external wall water pipes banged on with spoons bringing tenants together asking *"che success* (what happened)?" Mr. Georgio was missing! *Bocce,* m*oora,* and *briscola* card players talked more about *mala fortuna* (bad fortune) of Mr. Georgio then concentrating on their games.

Irish cops at Precinct #2 were notified. No one expected them to help because those "wop dagoes" were dating Irish girls. Tommy Smythe, an Irish police officer, cared. All of his off hours were given to finding Mr. Georgio.

Two day's after the loss, Stumbolucci's son, Alfredo, shouted *"Ho Truat! "Ho Truat! "Ho Truat!* I found him! I found him! I found him!

While on his way to PS #6, at 8:30 A.M. Alfred as usual performed his morning ritual. Cutting through the alleyway next to Marones Saloon, Alfredo would open the garbage shed to see big rats jump in and out of the garbage cans.

Alfredo noticed the wheelchair toppled over next to the garbage shed. The caned back of the wheelchair covered Mr. Giorgio. Alfredo went to find Bucky and Orlando.

What happened? Boys had pushed Mr. Georgio into the saloon alleyway and left him. Attempting to maneuver his way out with his right arm, the wheelchair rolled over a crumbled concrete protuberance. Mr. Georgio panicked and tried turning the right wheel, which slipped down a slight ramp and hit a broken bag of garbage. The wheelchair fell next to the shed, in between a growth of wild sumac (stink) trees. The caned chair fell over covering Mr. Georgio. Branches of the malleable sumac (stink) tree branches completely hid the chair. Mr. Georgio hit the concrete slab, bruised his face and laid in the middle of the broken bag of garbage. His groans were not heard.

Rats ran over him and under him to get to the broken, rotten smelling,

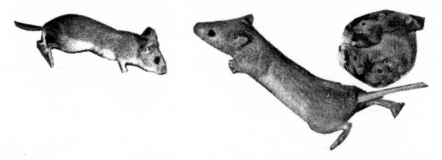

garbage bag. Rats ran along the saloon wall passing Mr. Georgio's face. Rats licked the spittle running down the sides of his lips and licked his tears dripping from his eyes and nostrils.

At Alfredo's screams, Bucky ran over and moved the wheelchair to an upright position. Then picked up his friend tenderly, holding him in his muscled arms. Bucky walked out of the alleyway. Mr. Georgio stayed embraced in a fetal position. His bruised, bloody face was totally red because of the shame he felt. Close eyed tears mingled with his mouth spittle covering his sticky, black beard. His pants were wet. His body odor was overwhelming. Mr. Georgio had peed and soiled his pants. The people watching this tender scene were teary eyed, saddened and quiet. No visable celebrations were considered. Cradling his friend, Bucky walked home. There were no more neighborhood rumors. This devastating, dark, happening hung through the neighborhood like black crape at a funeral mass.

Realizations of truth became apparent. Georgio had feelings like any other *Cristiano*. **Georgio Hurt!!** **Georgio Felt Shame!!** **Georgio Was Broken Hearted!!**

For months Mr. Georgio refused to leave his flat. There were no smiles, no responses, no glistening eyes. He remained mute.

Peppino continued to visit him twice per day. Untouched carob sticks laid in a bundle. Mr. Georgio's lowered head was above his fetal curled up body position.

On Christmas morning, Angelo visited other friends and Mr.

Georgio as was the Italian custom. Angelo was totally pleasantly surprised.

Mr. Georgio was clean shaven, sat in an upright position, and smiled with

glistening eyes. When he saw Angelo, he pointed to his brand new perfectly

fitting, patent leather, ox blood high top shoes.

About the Author

John is an accredited licensed certified social worker. Experiencing 45 years of work with the urban, poor he has published "The Abandoned Poor", a human rights spiritual case study manual complimenting many existing theoretical works.

Upon request of a professional periodical "People People" John has written a biography of a University of Buffalo dean of Social Work.

For the Mosignor Kerby Guild he published a review of "Mans Search for Meaning" and in collaboration with a Priest he published "Living the Catholic Mass trough Social Work." In Unison with Dr. and Mrs. Golden he has written an article "Crises Intervetion for Cardiac Patients" published in "Medical Insight" a magazine devoted to emotional factors in Medicine.

Printed in the United States
28684LVS00007B/36